THE ROYAL COURT
THEATRE PRESENTS

WHO CARES

BY MICHAEL WYNNE

Who Cares was first performed at the
Royal Court Jerwood Theatre Upstairs,
Sloane Square, on Friday 10 April 2015.

WHO CARES
BY MICHAEL WYNNE

CAST (in alphabetical order)

Philip Arditti Jonathon
Robert Bathurst Male Senior Consultant, Cardiologist,
Paul, Tony, Andrew Lansley, Jim
Elizabeth Berrington Cleaner, Louise, Julie
Paul Hickey Nurse, Carl, Cardiologist, Ex NHS Chief Executive, Peter
Martina Laird Female Consultant, Hannah, Cardiologist, Accountant One, Allyson
Nathaniel Martello-White Porter, Dave, Accountant Two, NHS Regulator
Eileen O'Brien Marjorie
Vineeta Rishi Junior Doctor, Lisa, Dr Malhotra, Jacky, Martina

STAFF & PATIENTS

Green Team
Clare Almond
Neil Anthony
Asha Cluer
Zhe Cui
Christopher Glover
Harriet Main

Blue Team
Lindon Alexander
Rahel Habtu
Ellen O'Connor
Mandy Rowland
Natasha Sivanandan
Dimitra Tennakoon

Directors **Debbie Hannan, Lucy Morrison, Hamish Pirie**
Designer **Andrew D Edwards**
Lighting Designer **Natasha Chivers**
Composer & Sound Designer **Daniel Krass**
Assistant Director **Roy Alexander Weise**
Casting Director **Amy Ball**
Creative Producer **Emily McLaughlin**
Production Manager **Ali Beale**
Costume Supervisor **Sabrina Cuniberto**
Stage Managers **Sophia Dalton, Nicola Donithorn, Julia Slienger**
Stage Management Work Placement **Hannah Phillips**
Set Constructed by **Ridiculous Solutions**

The Royal Court would like to thank all the people interviewed as part of the creation of this play.

The Royal Court & Stage Management wish to thank the following for their help with this production:
Ed Bennett at Southwest Medical, Hayley Dallimore, Marcelo dos Santos, Kim Gilchrist, Hampstead
Theatre, Gemma Kerr, Louise Stephens, Transcription City, UKS Mobility

WHO CARES
BY MICHAEL WYNNE

Michael Wynne (Writer)

For the Royal Court: **The Priory, The People are Friendly, The Knocky, The Red Flag (Theatre Local), Friday Night Sex (Open Court).**

Other theatre includes: **Sell Out, Dirty Wonderland (Frantic Assembly); The Boy Who Left Home (Actors Touring Company/tour); Tits/Teeth (Soho); Canvas (Chichester Festival); Hope Place (Liverpool Everyman).**

Television includes: **Substance, Where the Heart Is, Grafters, Reach for the Moon, As If, U Get Me, Eyes Down, Sugar Rush, Mayo, Little Crackers, Lapland, Being Eileen.**

Film includes: **My Summer of Love.**

Radio includes: **The Knocky.**

Awards include: **BAFTA for Best British Film, Evening Standard Film Award for Best Screenplay, The Michael Powell Award for Best British Film at the Edinburgh International Film Festival, Joint Winner of the Directors Guild Award for Best British Film (My Summer of Love); The Meyer Whitworth Prize (The Knocky); Time Out Award for Best Off-West End Production (Sell Out); Olivier Award for Best New Comedy (The Priory).**

Philip Arditti (Jonathon)

Theatre includes: **The Fourth Wise Man (Unicorn); Catch 22 (Northern Stage); Facts (Finborough); 66 Books (Bush); The Holy Rosenbergs, Blood & Gifts, England People Very Nice (National); Light Shining in Buckinghamshire, Silver Birch House, A Family Affair (Arcola); Rope (Almeida).**

Television includes: **Spotless, Humans, Ripper Street, The Honourable Woman, Strike Back, Game of Thrones, Da Vinci's Demons, Borgia, Twenty Twelve, Five Days, Father & Son, House of Saddam, 10 Days to War.**

Film includes: **The Danish Girl, Exodus: Gods & Kings, Hyena, Red 2, Leave to Remain, Singing Women, Wall, World War Z, Born of War, Interview with a Hitman, Women & Children, Happy–Go–Lucky.**

Radio includes: **Book at Bedtime: Gorsky, Farran at Bay, Reluctant Spy, Book of the Week: Then They Came for Me, Season of Migration to the North, Sugar & Snow, Snow, Happiness of Blond People, Points of Entry.**

Robert Bathurst (Male Senior Consultant, Cardiologist, Paul, Tony, Andrew Lansley, Jim)

Theatre includes: **Love, Loss & Chianti, An Ideal Husband, Getting Married (Chichester Festival); Blue/Orange (UK tour); Blithe Spirit (Theatre Royal, Bath/West End); Alex: The Stage Play (International tour); Whipping It Up (Bush/West End); Present Laughter (UK Tour); Alarms & Excursions (West End); Members Only (Trafalgar Studios); Three Sisters (West End); Hedda Gabler (Theatre Royal, Plymouth/UK tour); Good Copy (West Yorkshire Playhouse); The Rover, The Choice (Salisbury Playhouse); The Nose, The Comedy of Errors, The Importance of Being Earnest (Nottingham Playhouse); Noises Off (West End); Saint Joan, A Little Hotel on the Side, Injured Parties, Carrington (National); The Swap (Soho Boulevard); Judgement (Man in the Moon); Dry Rot (Theatre Royal, Bath/West End) The Next Best Thing (Nuffield, Southampton).**

Television includes: **Fleabag, Toast Of London, Downton Abbey, Cold Feet, Hattie, Joking Apart, White Teeth, Agatha Raisin, Cockroaches, Dracula, Blandings, Wild at Heart, The Pillars of the Earth, Emma, The Queen, Roman's Empire, My Family, Kingdom, Coup, Poirot, The Stepfather, The Odd Thing, The Secret, My Dad's The Prime Minister, White Teeth, Goodbye, Mr Steadman, Safe House, Loads of Tosh, Hornblower, Get Well Soon, A Breed of Heroes, The Lenny Henry Show, New World, Chelmsford 123, Blind Justice, Timeline, Anything More Would Be Greedy, Red Dwarf.**

Film includes: **Absolutely Anything, Narcopolis, Mrs Brown's Boys D'Movie, Heidi, The Thief Lord, The Wind in the Willows, Whoops Apocalypse, Just Ask for Diamond, Twenty-One.**

Ali Beale (Production Manager)

For the Royal Court: **Pests (& Clean Break/ Royal Exchange, Manchester).**

Other theatre includes: **Dusk, Above Me the Wide Blue Sky, It's the Skin You're Living In, The Forest, Brilliant, Stilled, An Infinite Line: Brighton, And the Rain Falls Down, The Summer Subversive, Fleet, The Field of Miracles, Feast Your Eyes (Fevered Sleep); Just Act, It Felt Empty, Missing Out, This Wide Night, Black Crows (Clean Break); Under Glass, Must, Performing Medicine, Sampled, Fantastic Voyage (The Clod Ensemble); Give Us a Hand! (The Little Angel); The Contents of a House, Guided Tour (Peter Reder); The Evocation of Papa Mas, The Firework Maker's Daughter, Aladdin, Playing the Victim, A Little Fantasy, Shoot Me in The Heart (Told by An Idiot); Gumbo Jumbo (The Gogmagogs); The Ratcatcher of Hamlin (Cartoon De Salvo); Oogly Boogly (Tom Morris/Guy Dartnell); Throat (Company FZ); Arcane (Opera Circus).**

Ali has worked with Fevered Sleep as Production Manager and Co-Designer since 2003.

Elizabeth Berrington (Cleaner, Louise, Julie)

For the Royal Court: **The Low Road, The Knocky.**

Other theatre includes: **Holes (Arcola); Absent Friends (West End); Abigail's Party (Hampstead); Top Girls (Oxford Stage Company); The Country Wife (Sheffield Crucible); An Ideal Husband (Royal Exchange, Manchester); The Left-Over Heart (Offstage Downstairs); Rupert Street Lonely Hearts Club (ETT tour/Donmar/The Criterion).**

Television includes: **The Syndicate, Pramface, Cuckoo, Midsomer Murders: Christmas Special, Stage Door Johnnies, Babylon, The Smoke, Trying Again, New Tricks, Stella, Lapland, Doctor Who, The Crimson Petal & the White, Waterloo Road, Psychoville, Jo Brand's Little Cracker, Moving Wallpaper, A Touch of Frost, Apparitions, Agatha Christie's Poirot, May Contain Nuts, Annually Retentive, Drop Dead Gorgeous, Love Lies Bleeding, Rose & Maloney, Missing, The Rotters Club, Where the Heart Is, Shane, Family Business, The Deal, Bodily Harm, Rescue Me, The Chambers, The Bill, Sam's Game, The Grimley's, The Vice, Let Them Eat Cake, Nature Boy, Casualty, The Lakes, My Wonderful Life, The Moonstone, Nurses, Between the Lines.**

Film includes: **Saturday, The Alan Partridge Movie, Mr Turner, Hard Boiled Sweets, In Bruges, Fred Claus, Are You Ready for Love, I Could Never Be Your Woman, Scoop, Nanny McPhee, A Cock & Bull Story, Vera Drake, Spivs, Quills, Little Vampires, Mad Cows, 8 ½ Women, Eugene Onegin, An Urban Ghost Story, Naked, Secrets & Lies.**

Radio includes: **Normal & Nat, Splash, Weird Tales.**

Natasha Chivers (Lighting Designer)

For the Royal Court: **Fireworks, Adler & Gibb, The Mistress Contract, Gastronauts, The Djinns of Eidgah, That Face (& West End).**

Other theatre includes: **Scuttlers (Royal Exchange, Manchester); Juno & The Paycock (Bristol Old Vic/Liverpool Playhouse); 1984 (Headlong/Almeida/ West End); Macbeth (National Theatre of Scotland/Broadway); The Green Snake (National Theatre of China); Praxis Makes Perfect (Neon Neon/National Theatre Wales); The Radicalisation Of Bradley Manning (National Theatre Wales); 27, The Wheel, Home: Glasgow, Mary Stuart, The House of Bernard Alba, Empty/The Miracle Man (National Theatre of Scotland); Boeing Boeing, One Monkey Don't Stop No Show, The Village Bike, Happy Days (Crucible, Sheffield); And The Horse You Rode in On (Told By An Idiot); Statement of Regret (National); Sunday in the Park with George (West End); The Wolves in the Walls (National Theatre of Scotland/Improbable); Othello, Dirty Wonderland, pool (no water), Tiny Dynamite, Peepshow, Hymns, Sell-Out (Frantic Assembly).**

Dance includes: **The Talent - Ballet Boyz (Linbury Theatre); Motor Show (LIFT/Brighton Festival); Electric Hotel (Sadler's Wells/Fuel); Electric Counterpoint (Royal Opera House); God's Garden (Arthur Pita/ROH Linbury/tour); Scattered, Broken (Motionhouse/tour/ Queen Elizabeth Hall); Run!, Renaissance (Greenwich & Docklands International Festival); Beyond Belief (Legs on the Wall/Carriageworks, Sydney);**

Encore (Sadler's Wells) The Ballet Boyz (Royal Festival Hall).

Awards include: **Olivier Award for Best Lighting Design (Sunday in the Park with George); UK Theatre Award 2011 for Best Design (Happy Days – with Lizzie Clachan); Theatre Critics of Wales Award 2014 for Best Lighting Design (Praxis Makes Perfect).**

Andrew D Edwards (Designer)

Theatre includes: **Romeo & Juliet (Globe/ Clwyd); The Life & Times of Fanny Hill (Bristol Old Vic); 101 Dalmatians, Miss Julie/Black Comedy, Blue Remembered Hills, Playhouse Creatures, Fred's Diner (Chichester Festival); Backbeat (West End/International tour); Les Parents Terribles (Donmar/Trafalgar Studios); Donny's Brain (Hampstead); A Voyage Around My Father (Salisbury Playhouse); Quiz Show (Traverse); Jesus Christ Superstar (Madrid/European tour); Measure For Measure (Theatre Royal, Plymouth/tour); Single Spies, Heroes, Educating Rita, Lettice & Lovage (Watermill); The Dumb Waiter (The Print Room); The Increased Difficulty of Concentration (Gate); The Speed Twins (Riverside Studio); No, It Was You (Arcola); The Smallest Thing (The Place).**

Dance includes: **Nanny McPhee (London Children's Ballet, Peacock).**

Debbie Hannan (Director)

As Director, for the Royal Court: **Peckham: The Soap Opera (co-director).**

As Assistant Director, for the Royal Court: **How to Hold Your Breath, God Bless the Child, Teh Internet is Serious Business, The Nether, Primetime, Birdland, The Mistress Contract.**

As Director, other theatre includes: **Notes from the Underground (Citizens); Woman of the Year (Oran Mor); Panorama, Roses Are Dead, You Cannot Call it Love (Arches); Yellow Pears (Swept Up); liberty, equality, fraternity (Tron/ Traverse)**

As Associate Director, other theatre includes: **Little on the Inside (Clean Break).**

As Assistant Director, other theatre includes: **A Doll's House, Enquirer (National Theatre of Scotland/Lyceum); The Maids, Beauty & the Beast (Citizens); Kurt Weill: Double Bill (Scottish Opera);**

War of the Roses Trilogy (Bard in the Botanics); Hamlet (Globe Education).

Paul Hickey (Nurse, Carl, Cardiologist, Ex NHS Chief Executive, Peter)

For the Royal Court: **Bang Bang Bang, O Go My Man (&Out of Joint), Fewer Emergencies, Crazyblackmotherfuckingself.**

Other theatre includes: **Little Light (Orange Tree); Incognito (Bush/HighTide); The Last Yankee (The Print Room); Children of the Sun, Our Class, Peer Gynt, Romeo & Juliet, Playboy of the Western World (National); Fred's Diner, Wallenstein (Chichester Festival); In the Next Room (Ustinov, Bath); Ghosts (Arcola); Fall (Traverse); Protestants (Soho); Aristocrats, Howling Moon Silent Sons, The Plough & the Stars, The Silver Tassie (Abbey, Dublin); Shiver, Spokesong (Rough Magic); Dealer's Choice, My Night With Reg (Birmingham Rep); The Merchant of Venice (RSC/International tour); Pentacost, In A Little World of Our Own (Donmar); Drink, Dance, Laugh, Lie (Bush); Deep Blue Sea (Royal Exchange, Manchester); Red Roses & Petrol, Lady Windemere's Fan, The Ash Fire (Tricycle).**

Television includes: **Critical, Doctor Who, Sunshine, Whitechapel, The Inspector Lynley Mysteries, Nuremberg, Friends & Crocodiles, Murder City, Rebel Heart, Father Ted, The Informant, The Governor.**

Film includes: **A Hundred Streets, Noble, The Devil's Harvest, On the Edge, Though The Sky Falls, Nora, Ordinary Decent Criminal, Saving Private Ryan, The General, The American, The Matchmaker, Moll Flanders.**

Danny Krass (Sound Designer)

Theatre includes: **Spoiling, The Artist Man & the Mother Woman, Quiz Show, The Devil Masters (Traverse); Up To Speed (Imaginate/Ros Sydney); The Adventures of Robin Hood (Visible Fictions/Kennedy Centre); The Voice Thief, Stuck, The Ballad of Pondlife McGurk, White, Kes (Catherine Wheels); My House, A Small Story (Starcatchers); Peter Pan (Sherman Cymru); Skewered Snails, He-La (Iron Oxide); Mikey & Addie, Littlest Christmas Tree, Rudolf, Mr Snow,**

The Little Boy that Santa Claus Forgot (Macrobert); The Infamous Brothers Davenport (Vox Motus/Royal Lyceum, Edinburgh); One Thousand Paper Cranes (Lu Kemp); The Curious Scrapbook of Josephine Bean, Huff (& Shona Reppe Puppets), The Day I Swapped My Dad for Two Goldfish, The Tin Forest Govan, South West (National Theatre of Scotland); Couldn't Care Less (Plutôt la Vie/Strange); Sanitise (Melanie Jordan); Smokies (Solar Bear).

Martina Laird (Female Consultant, Hannah, Cardiologist, Accountant One, Allyson)

For the Royal Court: **Breath, Boom.**

Other theatre includes: **The House That Will Not Stand** (Tricycle); **Moon on a Rainbow Shawl** (National/UK tour); **Hopelessly Devoted** (Birmingham Rep); **Inheritance** (Live!); **All the Little Things We Crushed** (Almeida); **Bad Blood Blues** (Theatre Royal, Stratford East); **Mules** (Young Vic); **Othello** (Donmar); **The Five Wives of Maurice Pinder** (National); **Arabian Knights** (West End/International tour); **Hyacinth Blue** (Clean Break); **The White Devil, Three Hours After Marriage, Troilus & Cressida** (RSC); **Venetian Heat** (Finborough); **Hungry Ghosts** (Tabard); **Vibes From Scribes** (Double Edge); **The Max King** (Man in the Moon).

Television includes: **The Dumping Ground, London's Burning, Coronation Street, Doctors, My Family, Missing, Shameless, Free Agents, Monday Monday, Casualty, Little Big Mouth, A Touch of Frost, Always & Everyone, The Bill, A Wing & a Prayer, Peak Practice, Jonathan Creek, Dangerfield, Thief Takers, The Knock, The Governor, One for the Road, Little Napoleons, Harry, West Indian Women at War, EastEnders, Epiphany.**

Film includes: **Blitz, Forget Me Not, The Hurting.**

Nathaniel Martello-White (Porter, Dave, Accountant Two, NHS Regulator)

For the Royal Court: **Teh Internet is Serious Business, The Get Out, Gastronauts, Oxford Street.**

Other theatre includes: **Edward II** (National); **City Madame, A Midsummer Night's Dream, Marat/Sade** (RSC); **Innocence, Knives in Hens** (Arcola);

Joe Turner's Come & Gone, Blackta (& writer) (Young Vic); Bad Blood Blues (Theatre Royal, Stratford East); The Brothers Size (Actors Touring Company/Young Vic); Romeo & Juliet (National/tour).

Television includes: **Silk, Death in Paradise, Misfits, Katy Brand's Big Ass Show, Law & Order: UK, Channel 4 Comedy Lab, Mongrels, Coming Up, Roman Mysteries, Doctors, Party Animals, Trial & Retribution.**

Film includes: **Hard Boiled Sweets, Life Just Is, Red Tails, Sisterhood of the Travelling Pants 2, The Preacher, Deadmeat, Heat, Invisible.**

Lucy Morrison (Director)

For the Royal Court: **Pests** (& Royal Exchange, Manchester/Clean Break); **Product** (& Traverse/European tour).

Other theatre includes: **Little on the inside** (Almeida/Edinburgh International Festival/Clean Break); **Billy the Girl** (Clean Break/Soho); **it felt empty when the heart went at first but it is alright now** (Arcola/Clean Break); **This Wide Night** (Soho/Live!/Clean Break); **This Wide Night** (Soho/Live!/Drum, Plymouth); **Fatal Light, Doris** (Soho); **Housekeeping** (Southwark/Latitude Festival).

Lucy was formerly Head of Artistic Programme at Clean Break and Literary Manager of Plaines Plough. She is now an Associate Director at the Royal Court.

Eileen O'Brien (Marjorie)

For the Royal Court: **The Knocky, Redundant.**

Other theatre includes: **Sex & the Three Day Week** (Liverpool Playhouse); **Hope Place, Macbeth, 'Tis Pity She's a Whore, Rag & Bone** (Everyman, Liverpool); **Forget Me Not** (Belvoir, Sydney); **What You Will: Pop up Shakespeare** (Globe); **The Revenger's Tragedy, Basil & Beattie, Across Oka, Rafts & Dreams, Yerma, Prize Night, The Plough & the Stars** (Royal Exchange, Manchester); **We Are Three Sisters, Richard III** (No. 1 tour/Northern Broadsides); **When We Are Married** (West Yorkshire Playhouse/Liverpool Playhouse); **Death of a Salesman** (York Theatre Royal); **An Inspector Calls** (Oldham Coliseum); **The Crucible, The Beauty Queen of Leenane** (Bolton Octagon); **Kindertransport, A Doll's House** (Shared Experience); **Foxes,**

Enjoy (West Yorkshire Playhouse); On the Shore of the Wide World (National/Royal Exchange, Manchester); Beyond Belief, Death of a Salesman (Manchester Library); Absent Friends, Bedroom Farce, Confusion (Stephen Joseph, Scarborough).

Television includes: **Holby City, Led Astray, Doctors, Emmerdale, Being Eileen, Lennon Naked, Moving On, Origins & Evolution, Red in Tooth & Claw, The Royal Today, Casualty, A Touch of Frost, Building the Titanic, Eyes Down, The Royal, Merseybeat, The Vice, Brookside, The Life & Crimes of William Palmer, The Practice, And the Beat Goes On, No Bananas, Rockliffe's Babies, One in a Thousand, Last Company Car, The Nation's Health, Boys from the Blackstuff, The Sheik of Pickersgill, The Crezz.**

Film includes: **Before Dawn, Fanny & Elvis, A Private Function, A Month in the Country, Runners, Between Two Women.**

Radio includes: **The Diddakoi, The Judas Burner, I.D, Legacy, Caligari, Tin Man, Snow In July, Sangam Restaurant: Mushroom Pakora, Stages of Sound: Silver Grey, The Changing Room, The Voyage Out, Driftwood Heart, Car 5, East Coast Girls Are Hip, Baloney Said Salome, The Morning After, Tell Me A Film, Red Rock Grey Rock.**

Awards include: **Liverpool Daily Post Award for Best Actress (Rag & Bone); Manchester Evening News Award for Best Actress (The Plough & the Stars); Manchester Evening News Award for Best Actress (The Beauty Queen of Leenane).**

Hamish Pirie (Director)

For the Royal Court: **Teh Internet is Serious Business.**

Other theatre includes: **I'm With The Band (Traverse/Wales Millennium Centre); Quiz Show, Demos, 50 Plays for Edinburgh (Traverse); Love With A Capital 'L', 3 Seconds, Most Favoured, The Last Bloom (Traverse/Òran Mór); Bravo Figaro (Royal Opera House/Traverse); Salt Root & Roe (Donmar/Trafalgar Studios); Purgatory (Arcola); Stacy (Arcola/Trafalgar); Pennies (nabokov); Paper House (Flight 5065).**

Hamish trained as Resident Assistant Director at Paines Plough & at the Donmar Warehouse. He was previously Associate Director at the Traverse Theatre. Hamish is an Associate Director at the Royal Court.

Vineeta Rishi (Junior Doctor, Lisa, Dr Malhotra, Jacky, Martina)

Theatre includes: **The House of Bilquis Bibi (Tamasha); There's Something About Simmy (Rifco); Weights (Merco); What We Did to Weinstein (Menier Chocolate Factory); Beasts & Beauties (Bristol Old Vic); Hobson's Choice (Young Vic); Beyond the Wall, The Firebird (Midlands Arts); The Tempest (1399); Picture Me (Red Ladder); Daisy Pulls It Off (People's).**

Television includes: **Boy Meets Girl, Doctors, Waking the Dead, Criminal Justice, Outnumbered, Heroes & Villains: Cortes, Doctor Who, Berry's Way, Where The Heart Is, The Last Detective, Lawless, The Bill.**

Radio includes: **Pilgrim, Karma, Haunted, Lights Out, The Far Pavilions, The Last Witch Trial, High Hopes, We Outnumber You, The Contingency Plan.**

Roy Alexander Weise
(Assistant Director)

As Assistant Director, for the Royal Court: **Liberian Girl.**

As Director, other theatre includes: **Plunder, One Million Tiny Plays About Britain (Young Vic); Palindrome, Miniaturists 50 (Arcola); The Man in the Green Jacket (Jermyn Street); What Happens Behind the Bar (The Cockpit); SKEEN! (Ovalhouse); Invisible Mice, The Ugly One (Lyric, Hammersmith); Seventeen (The Barn); Chameleon (Unicorn).**

As Assistant Director, other theatre includes: **Albion (Bush); We Are Proud to Present a Presentation of the Herero of Namibia Formerly Known as Southwest Africa of the German Sudwestafrika Between the Years 1884 & 1915 (Bush); Public Enemy, Hamlet, The Government Inspector (Young Vic); The Serpent's Tooth (Shoreditch Town Hall/Almeida/Talawa); Lulu (The Barn).**

Roy is currently the Trainee Director at the Royal Court.

THE ROYAL COURT THEATRE

The Royal Court Theatre is the writers' theatre. It is the leading force in world theatre for energetically cultivating writers – undiscovered, new, and established.

Through the writers the Royal Court is at the forefront of creating restless, alert, provocative theatre about now, inspiring audiences and influencing future writers. Through the writers the Royal Court strives to constantly reinvent the theatre ecology, creating theatre for everyone.

We invite and enable conversation and debate, allowing writers and their ideas to reach and resonate beyond the stage, and the public to share in the thinking.

Over 120,000 people visit the Royal Court in Sloane Square, London, each year and many thousands more see our work elsewhere through transfers to the West End and New York, national and international tours, residencies across London and site-specific work.

The Royal Court's extensive development activity encompasses a diverse range of writers and artists and includes an ongoing programme of writers' attachments, readings, workshops and playwriting groups. Twenty years of pioneering work around the world means the Royal Court has relationships with writers on every continent.

The Royal Court opens its doors to radical thinking and provocative discussion, and to the unheard voices and free thinkers that, through their writing, change our way of seeing.

Within the past sixty years, John Osborne, Arnold Wesker and Howard Brenton have all started their careers at the Court. Many others, including Caryl Churchill, Mark Ravenhill and Sarah Kane have followed. More recently, the theatre has found and fostered new writers such as Polly Stenham, Mike Bartlett, Bola Agbaje, Nick Payne and Rachel De-lahay and produced many iconic plays from Laura Wade's **Posh** to Bruce Norris' **Clybourne Park** and Jez Butterworth's **Jerusalem**. Royal Court plays from every decade are now performed on stage and taught in classrooms across the globe.

It is because of this commitment to the writer that we believe there is no more important theatre in the world than the Royal Court.

Supported using public funding by
ARTS COUNCIL ENGLAND

MAY – JUL 2015

JERWOOD THEATRE UPSTAIRS

3 Jun - 11 Jul
Violence and Son
by Gary Owen

An intimate new play about what parents pass on and trying to do the right thing.

18 Jul - 25 Jul
Primetime

A series of new short plays written by primary school children aged eight to 11.

Primetime is supported by John Lyon's Charity, The Mercers' Company, John Thaw Foundation, and The Austin and Hope Pilkington Trust.

JERWOOD THEATRE DOWNSTAIRS

11 Jun - 18 Jul
hang
written and directed by debbie tucker green

A shattering new play about an unspeakable decision.

ON TOUR

14 May – 4 Jul
Constellations
by Nick Payne

★★★★★
"Extraordinary. Dazzling."
Independent

NEW VICTORIA THEATRE (WOKING), LIVERPOOL PLAYHOUSE, BRISTOL OLD VIC, NUFFIELD THEATRE (SOUTHAMPTON), THE LOWRY (SALFORD QUAYS), CAMBRIDGE ARTS THEATRE, RICHMOND THEATRE, THEATRE ROYAL BRIGHTON.

Constellations was first staged in 2012 as part of the Royal Court's Jerwood New Playwrights programme, supported by Jerwood Charitable Foundation.

2 – 7 Jun
Not I / Footfalls / Rockaby
by Samuel Beckett

★★★★★
"Stunning. Moving. Chilling."
Daily Telegraph

BARBICAN CENTRE

Presented by the Royal Court Theatre and Lisa Dwan in association with Cusack Projects Ltd.

WEST END

Until 25 Apr
The Nether
by Jennifer Haley

★★★★★
"Mind-bending... Ingenious"
The Times

DUKE OF YORK'S THEATRE

A Headlong and Royal Court Theatre co-production. Presented by Sonia Friedman Productions and Scott M Delman in association with Tulchin Bartner Productions, Lee Dean & Charles Diamond, 1001 Nights, JFL Theatricals/GHF Productions, Scott + Brian Zellinger / James Lefkowitz.

020 7565 5000 (no booking fee)
royalcourttheatre.com

Follow us 🐦 royalcourt 📘 royalcourttheatre
Royal Court Theatre Sloane Square London, SW1W 8AS

ROYAL COURT SUPPORTERS

The Royal Court is a registered charity and not-for-profit company. We need to raise £1.7 million every year in addition to our core grant from the Arts Council and our ticket income to achieve what we do.

We have significant and longstanding relationships with many generous organisations and individuals who provide vital support. Royal Court supporters enable us to remain the writers' theatre, find stories from everywhere and create theatre for everyone.

We can't do it without you.

Coutts supports Innovation at the Royal Court. The Genesis Foundation supports the Royal Court's work with International Playwrights. Alix Partners support The Big Idea at the Royal Court. Bloomberg supports Beyond the Court. The Jerwood Charitable Foundation supports emerging writers through the Jerwood New Playwrights series. The Pinter Commission is given annually by his widow, Lady Antonia Fraser, to support a new commission at the Royal Court.

PUBLIC FUNDING

Arts Council England, London
British Council

CHARITABLE DONATIONS

The Austin & Hope
  Pilkington Trust
Martin Bowley Charitable Trust
Cowley Charitable Trust
The Dorset Foundation
The Eranda Foundation
Lady Antonia Fraser for
  The Pinter Commission
Genesis Foundation

The Golden Bottle Trust
The Haberdashers' Company
Roderick & Elizabeth Jack
Jerwood Charitable
Foundation
Marina Kleinwort Trust
The Andrew Lloyd Webber
Foundation
John Lyon's Charity
Clare McIntyre's Bursary
The Andrew W. Mellon
Foundation
The Mercers' Company
The David & Elaine Potter
Foundation
Rose Foundation
Royal Victoria Hall Foundation
The Sackler Trust
The Sobell Foundation
John Thaw Foundation
The Vandervell Foundation
Sir Siegmund Warburg's
Voluntary Settlement
The Garfield Weston
Foundation
The Wolfson Foundation

CORPORATE SPONSORS

AKA
AlixPartners
Aqua Financial Solutions Ltd
Bloomberg
Colbert
Coutts
Fever-Tree
Gedye & Sons
MAC
Nyetimber

BUSINESS MEMBERS

Annoushka
Auerbach & Steele
  Opticians
CNC – Communications &
  Network Consulting
Cream
Heal's
Lazard
Salamanca Group
Tetragon Financial Group
Vanity Fair

DEVELOPMENT ADVOCATES

Piers Butler
Sindy Caplan
Sarah Chappatte
Cas Donald (Vice Chair)
Celeste Fenichel
Piers Gibson
Emma Marsh (Chair)
Deborah Shaw
  (Vice Chair)
Tom Siebens
Sian Westerman

INDIVIDUAL SUPPORTERS

Major Donors

Eric Abraham
Ray Barrell & Ursula Van Almsick
Cas Donald
Lydia & Manfred Gorvy
Richard & Marcia Grand
Jack & Linda Keenan
Adam Kenwright
Mandeep Manku
Miles Morland
Mr & Mrs Sandy Orr
NoraLee & Jon Sedmak
Deborah Shaw & Stephen Marquardt
Jan & Michael Topham
Monica B Voldstad

Mover-Shakers

Anonymous
Jordan Cook
Piers & Melanie Gibson
Duncan Matthews QC
Ian & Carol Sellars

Boundary-Breakers

Anonymous
Katie Bradford
David Harding
Madeleine Hodgkin
Roderick & Elizabeth Jack
Nicola Kerr
Philip & Joan Kingsley
Emma Marsh
Rachel Mason
Angelie Moledina
Andrew & Ariana Rodger

Ground-Breakers

Anonymous
Moira Andreae
Mr & Mrs Simon Andrews
Nick Archdale
Elizabeth & Adam Bandeen
Michael Bennett
Sam & Rosie Berwick
Dr Kate Best
Christopher Bevan
Sarah & David Blomfield
Deborah Brett
Peter & Romey Brown
Clive & Helena Butler
Piers Butler

Sindy & Jonathan Caplan
Gavin & Lesley Casey
Sarah & Philippe Chappatte
Tim & Caroline Clark
Carole & Neville Conrad
Clyde Cooper
Ian & Caroline Cormack
Mr & Mrs Cross
Andrew & Amanda Cryer
Alison Davies
Roger & Alison De Haan
Matthew Dean
Sarah Denning
Polly Devlin OBE
Rob & Cherry Dickins
Denise & Randolph Dumas
Robyn Durie
Glenn & Phyllida Earle
Graham & Susanna Edwards
Mark & Sarah Evans
Sally & Giles Everist
Celeste & Peter Fenichel
Margy Fenwick
The Edwin Fox Foundation
Dominic & Claire Freemantle
Beverley Gee
Nick & Julie Gould
Lord & Lady Grabiner
Jill Hackel & Andrzej Zarzycki
Carol Hall
Maureen Harrison
Sam & Caroline Haubold
Mr & Mrs Gordon Holmes
Kate Hudspeth
Damien Hyland
Suzie & David Hyman
Amanda & Chris Jennings
Melanie J Johnson
Nicholas Jones
Susanne Kapoor
David P Kaskel
  & Christopher A Teano
Vincent & Amanda Keaveny
Peter & Maria Kellner
Steve Kingshott
Mr & Mrs Pawel Kisielewski
David & Sarah Kowitz
Daisy & Richard Littler
Kathryn Ludlow
Suzanne Mackie
Dr Ekaterina Malievskaia
  & George Goldsmith
Christopher Marek Rencki
Mr & Mrs Marsden
Mrs Janet Martin
Andrew McIver

David & Elizabeth Miles
Barbara Minto
Takehito Mitsui
M. Murphy Altschuler
Peter & Maggie Murray-Smith
Ann & Gavin Neath CBE
Clive & Annie Norton
Kate O'Neill
Jonathan Och & Rita Halbright
Georgia Oetker
Adam Oliver-Watkins
Anatol Orient
Sir William & Lady Vanessa Patey
Andrea & Hilary Ponti
Annie & Preben Prebensen
Greg & Karen Reid
Paul & Gill Robinson
Daniel Romualdez
Sir Paul & Lady Ruddock
William & Hilary Russell
Sally & Anthony Salz
Bhags Sharma
Tom Siebens & Mimi Parsons
Andy Simpkin
Brian Smith
Saadi & Zeina Soudavar
The Ulrich Family
Constanze Von Unruh
Matthew & Sian Westerman
Mrs Alexandra Whiley
Anne-Marie Williams
Sir Robert & Lady Wilson
Katherine & Michael Yates

With thanks to our Friends, Stage-Taker, Ice-Breaker and Future Court members whose support we greatly appreciate.

Innovation partner

Supported using public funding by

ARTS COUNCIL ENGLAND

Support the world's leading new writing theatre

By making a donation to the Royal Court you can help us to respond to new and established playwrights, and supply them with the time, resources and environment to follow their imagination and exceed their potential.

As well as nurturing writers, we rely on the donations we receive to make all our work, on stage and off, happen- from playwriting groups through to access initiatives, subsidised tickets, schools tours, workshops, festivals and productions.

A gift from you, no matter how big or small, can help the Royal Court to ensure its ongoing success and change theatre forever.

MAKE A DONATION

To make a donation to the Royal Court, please:

Call Anna Sampson on 020 7565 5049
Email annasampson@royalcourttheatre.com
Visit royalcourttheatre.com/donations

You can also text 'PLAYS' to 70099 to donate £3.
(£3 charge +1 message @ your standard network rate. 100% of your donation will be received by the Royal Court, thank you.)

Who Cares

Michael Wynne was born and brought up in Birkenhead.
His first play *The Knocky* (Meyer Whitworth Award -
Best New Playwright and Best New Writer Nomination –
Writers' Guild) was produced by the Royal Court. His
other credits for the Royal Court include *The Priory*
(Olivier Award – Best New Comedy), *The People Are
Friendly*, *The Red Flag* and *Friday Night Sex*. Wynne's
work also includes the first new play at the rebuilt
Liverpool Everyman, *Hope Place*, and *Canvas* (Minerva
Theatre, Chichester), *Sell Out* (Best Off West End – *Time
Out* Theatre Awards) and *Dirty Wonderland* (both
Frantic Assembly), *Tits/Teeth* (Soho Theatre) and *The
Boy Who Left Home* (Actors Touring Company). He has
also written extensively for screen, including *My Summer
of Love* (BAFTA – Best British Film, *Evening Standard*
Film Awards – Best Screenplay, The Michael Powell
Award for Best British Film at the Edinburgh Film
Festival, joint winner of the Directors' Guild Award for
Best British Film), *Lapland* and *Being Eileen* for the BBC.

also by Michael Wynne from Faber

THE KNOCKY
THE PRIORY
THE PEOPLE ARE FRIENDLY
CANVAS
HOPE PLACE

MICHAEL WYNNE

Who Cares

FABER & FABER

First published in 2015

by Faber and Faber Limited
74–77 Great Russell Street, London WC1B 3DA

Typeset by Country Setting, Kingsdown, Kent CT14 8ES
Printed in England by CPI Group (UK) Ltd, Croydon CR0 4YY

A CIP record for this book is available from the British Library

ISBN 978-0-571-32640-2

FSC
www.fsc.org
MIX
Paper from
responsible sources
FSC® C013604

2 4 6 8 10 9 7 5 3 1

Acknowledgements

Who Cares has been edited, shaped and framed from interviews conducted by Michael Wynne over eighteen months with people working in and around the National Health Service. It includes the words of some, but not all, of the people listed below.

Kathryn Anderson, Julie Bailey, Andrea Bamford, Christopher Bamford, Peter Bamford, Hannah Bishop, Marjorie Boukhari, Mark Britnell, Steven Bubb, Andy Burnham, Thomas Cawston, Kailash Chand, Anita Charlesworth, Frederic Chiles, Karen Chilver, Marcus Chown, Tony Corner, Paul Corrigan, India Crawford Legg, Jacky Davis, Peter Diem, Liam Donaldson, Jim Easton, Bob Gill, Lisa Humfress, Louise Irvine, Sofie Karlsson, Julien Le Grand, Caroline Leverett, Aseem Malhotra, Anne McElvoy, John Myatt, David Nicholson, Clive Peedell, Allyson Pollock, David Skidmore, Richard Taylor, Roger Taylor, Jonathan Tomlinson, Martina Wade, David Wrigley, Alyson Yandoli, Dennis Yandoli.

I would like to say a huge thank you to all the above for their time, passion and wisdom. The play would not exist without their words.

I would also like to thank Alecky Blythe, Andra Flavia Catinescu, Emily McLaughlin, Chris James, Elyse Dodgson, Louise Stephens, Minna Sharpe, Kevin O Kane, Bobby Ganger, Michael McCoy, Paul Keating, Maureen Beattie, Julie Graham, Karl Johnson, Elliot Levey, Aisling Loftus, Nicolas Tennant, Debra Oswald, Debbie Hannan, Lucy Morrison, Hamish Pirie, Roy Alexander Weise, Vicky Featherstone, Lucy Davies, David Hare and all at the Royal Court who made this production possible.

Who Cares was first produced in the Jerwood Theatre Upstairs at the Royal Court Theatre, London, on 10 April 2015. The cast was as follows:

Jonathon Philip Arditti
Male Senior Consultant, Cardiologist, Paul, Tony, Andrew Lansley, Jim Robert Bathurst
Cleaner, Louise, Julie Elizabeth Berrington
Nurse, Carl, Cardiologist, Ex-NHS Chief Executive, Peter Paul Hickey
Female Consultant, Hannah, Cardiologist, Accountant One, Allyson Martina Laird
Porter, Dave, Accountant Two, NHS Regulator Nathaniel Martello-White
Marjorie Eileen O'Brien
Junior Doctor, Lisa, Dr Malhotra, Jacky, Martina Vineeta Rishi

STAFF AND PATIENTS
Green Team Clare Almond, Neil Anthony, Asha Cluer, Zhe Cui, Christopher Glover, Harriet Main
Blue Team Lindon Alexander, Rahel Habtu, Ellen O'Connor, Mandy Rowland, Natasha Sivanandan, Dimitra Tennakoon

Directors Debbie Hannan, Lucy Morrison, Hamish Pirie
Designer Andrew D. Edwards
Lighting Designer Natasha Chivers
Composer and Sound Designer Daniel Krass
Assistant Director Roy Alexander Weise
Casting Director Amy Ball
Costume Supervisor Sabrina Cuniberto

Characters

in order of appearance

Marjorie

Female Consultant

Cleaner

Senior Consultant

Nurse

Junior Doctor

Porter

Man with iPad

Drunk Woman

Drunk Man

Jonathon

Hannah

Carl

Lisa

Louise

Dave

Cardiologist

Two Accountants

Dr Malhotra

Ex-NHS Chief Exec

Ex-Department of Health National Director

Allyson

Paul

Jacky

NHS Regulator

Julie Bailey

Peter Bamford

Martina

Tony

Andrew Lansley MP

Jim

Anita

WHO CARES

Act One: Symptoms

As we enter we're greeted by two smokers on drips in wheelchairs and pyjamas.

A hyper-real Accident & Emergency waiting room.

The entrance on one side, and a door off to triage, resus, majors, AAU, paediatrics on the opposite side. Plastic chairs all round the room, signs and notices to other departments.

Large flatscreen TV. Jeremy Kyle Show *on – with subtitles for hard of hearing – 'Leave your violent partner – he tried to inject me with heroin.'*

Lots of posters and notices:

CLEAN HANDS SAVE LIVES.

PATIENT SATISFACTION. How was your visit today? Please fill in a form.

EBOLA IN WEST AFRICA. If you have returned from Guinea, Liberia and Sierra Leone or cared for someone with ebola in the past 21 days and you have a fever or feel unwell – without making physical contact, tell a member of staff.

Signs to: Osborne Ward, Churchill Ward, Butterworth Ward.

A ticket machine for patients to take their number. Occasional announcements – 'Ticket number 236 go to window 3.'

Doctors and nurses in different coloured uniforms pass through, rushed off their feet, emergencies coming in, noise and hubbub of a bustling NHS hospital.

A few patients already waiting.

An incredibly frail and bruised old lady on her own,
a drunk couple eating a burger and chips, a man in his
twenties with a tiny plaster on his finger and his iPad in
hand, a vulnerable-looking middle-aged woman, a
homeless man in hat and coat looking very dishevelled
surrounded by plastic bags.

Occasional sirens outside, children crying in paediatrics,
screams and shouting from elsewhere. It's busy, chaotic,
at times scary.

Marjorie, a sixty-year-old nurse from Yorkshire, appears.

Marjorie I started. I guess, when I was born. Or even in
the womb and things because my father was a male nurse,
so I was born into nursing, as it were. My childhood was
completely absorbed in hospital work. My father being
a charge nurse, would always put himself on duty at
Christmas time. The ward which was the old (*she laughs*)
Nightingale Ward was turned into a little banquet for the
patients and the relatives on a Christmas afternoon . . .
And I'd go along. I would go along. That would be my
Christmas Day. We'd get up in the morning before Dad
went on duty, get my presents open from Santa and then
in the afternoon, after lunch, we'd go and spend some
time with my father. And that set me off with the long-
term goal.

Female Consultant I think it's the emotions around the
NHS that are really, really interesting.

Over Tannoy: 'Housekeeping to cubicle nine, please.'

Junior Doctor A budget of just over a hundred billion a
year.

Cleaner Not a hundred million but a hundred billion!

Senior Consultant We have an institution which is unlike
any other, in that it's an institution which actually has,
sort of meaning up here (*points to head*) as well as
meaning down here (*points to heart*).

Nurse Resus full again and three waiting.

Cleaner If it was a country, it would be the 33rd largest country in the world, you know.

Female Consultant Need a purple, a yellow and a blue.

Junior Doctor There were two polls done at the millennium . . . 'What's the most important event of the 20th century?' Nearly 50 per cent said creating the NHS, and only 18 per cent said winning the Second World War.

Nurse He's on three-fifty. He's gonna breach.

Senior Consultant What's the most important institution of the country? 48 per cent the NHS, 12 per cent Parliament, 6 per cent monarchy. So it's sort of instinctively, when people think actually about defining who we are, it's sort of the NHS comes quite near the top.

Female Consultant CT in number 6.

Cleaner The NHS is the fifth largest employer in the world. 1.7 million workers. Just behind McDonald's, Walmart, the Chinese army, and the United States military at number one.

Marjorie When I was seven, I distinctly remember this, somebody asked me, 'And what are you going to be when you grow up?' And the answer came back, I remember, 'I'm going to be an SRN, a midwife, but I'm going to be a sister tutor,' which is what we used to call our educators, the teachers. 'And why do you want to be a sister tutor?' And I can remember, I'd thought this out, and this was my answer. 'Why? Because, when I'm retired and when I'm dead and gone, I can still be helping patients because all my students will be going out and they will be nursing their lifelong patients,' from their career experience and things.
So that was the answer . . .

Senior Consultant Somewhere in the middle of all this, it's a phrase that we used to use, it's the best gift the British people have given to themselves. Because it is, no one else has done this.

Porter One thing about the NHS is how huge it is and the scale of what it does. People will often just focus on the hospital, or the emergency, or whatever.

Man with iPad How much longer? I've now been waiting here for . . .

Female Consultant But it's massive. From looking after the high-secure hospitals, like Rampton, through to chiropody for older people. From disabled children to people who require liver transplants.

Porter There are 300 million GP consultations per year and 22 million A&E visits.

Female Consultant We get many frequent fliers. They go from hospital to hospital. Most of them know that if they say 'chest pains' we have to see them.

The drunk couple are getting very amorous, kissing, hands everywhere.

Drunk Woman Get off. Not here.

Drunk Man You want it.

She pushes him off. He looks around and starts on a nearby patient.

What you looking at? Eh? Look at me once more and I'll . . .

A paramedic wheels a patient through with bandaged and bloodied head.

Marjorie You can have coming through at any one time: the drunk being found off the street, doesn't have any identity with him. The psychotic that has been self-harming and things. A dear young woman, it's her first baby and he's miscarrying. You can have a cancer patient on a crisis in between the chemotherapy. Chest pain, somebody that's gone into cardiac arrest . . .

The vulnerable-looking woman start crying quietly.

So you've got everything coming through . . . on that . . . in that . . . through that one door.

Junior Doctor The problem – the fundamental problem of the Health Service, it's a victim of its own success.

Porter The NHS deals with a million patients every 36 hours.

Junior Doctor Neck up and check up. Call psych.

Senior Consultant I remember I worked for a time at the Royal Berkshire Hospital, and there was a ward called the West Ward that nobody ever wanted to go because it was the cancer ward. People didn't like going there because those who went in rarely came out, because there were no treatments for cancer.

Drunk Woman I feel sick. I'm gonna . . .

She goes off to throw up. We hear her vomiting off.

Nurse Whereas nowadays . . . you know, there are a dozen different treatments for prostate cancer, which – there were no treatments ten, twenty years ago.

Female Consultant And we're now doing deep brain stimulation procedures – you know, open skull procedures – on patients who are awake!

Phones ringing.

Junior Doctor He's gone to theatre.

Senior Consultant I just said to her, 'I think you might be having a heart attack.' She said, 'Can I go outside for a smoke?'

Cleaner Why do people call 999 when they shouldn't? Is it because we live in a 24-hour culture that demands everything now?

Senior Consultant Sick or not sick?

Nurse Not sick.

Senior Consultant Four-hour waits. In the old days, if you came to A&E with some bollocks complaint, you were at the end of the list and you stayed there till everyone more urgent had been seen. You'd soon get fed up of doing that.

Cleaner Cubicle nine is off. Needs a full deep clean.

Elderly Man (*off*) Help me, help me.

Female Consultant There's a sort of interface between what you've just got to get on and do every day, which is see patients, make life better for them, try and make them better, and somewhere up above you, the storms are raging, but you're not really aware of them because as long as you can actually do your job . . .

Senior Consultant What's her time?

Junior Doctor Three forty-three. They won't take her upstairs. She'll breach.

Female Consultant But when you poke your head through the surface and just see this huge storm raging up there, you think: 'Why didn't I know about that?'

Marjorie We're supposed to see everybody through in four hours . . . In and out, yeah. And get them off. Because it goes up on the computer. It will go up into a red zone to say, now you're breaching and you'll get penalised.

Nurse We can't take any more. We're full.

Marjorie If it goes into a red the department gets a fine.

Child (*crying, off*) Mummy! Mummy!

Marjorie If any . . . go down – like I say – if anybody wants a pee at three (*she laughs*) hours 57 minutes – because that spending a penny is going to cost the trust a fortune.

Female Consultant My mother has often said to me, 'I don't *really* understand how you can spend your whole life with ill people, it'd be too depressing.' She always thought that would be the most ghastly thing to have to do with your life: spend every day with people who were sick . . .

Nurse Let me get her a cup of tea.

Female Consultant And when you put it like that, you *do* wonder why . . . anybody would choose to do it! And you know that you can't make an awful lot of people that much better, unfortunately.

Senior Consultant I'm sending him home with a lozenge.

Junior Doctor Accident and emergency units – although you would think of them as very unpredictable, when you look at it there are very strong patterns. So lots of people turn up on a Monday. Been ill through the weekend, get to the beginning of the week, not feeling better, go in on a Monday morning. And everywhere across the country, Monday mornings are really busy in A&E.

On the TV screen adverts appear:
BACKACHE? *Don't go to A&E – go to GP.*
DIARRHOEA? *Don't go to A&E – go to pharmacy.*
SORE THROAT? *Don't go to A&E – go to pharmacy.*
Use notalwaysAandE.co.uk

Senior Consultant It's a bit like King Canute, trying to stop patients accessing healthcare is, is a forlorn hope – you may be able to direct them a little bit, but the public are not stupid, and particularly the younger population, they don't want to wait two or three days to see a GP – neither do I.

Jonathon, a North London GP, appears.

Jonathon I had appendicitis in 1999 . . . and I was in London when it started and I was junior surgeon at the time and I'd done nearly six months of surgery, so seen loads of cases of appendicitis and I thought it was just psychosomatic.

So I got on a train and went to Glasgow . . .

The homeless man starts moaning in pain.

Then I got really sick and thought 'Oh I don't feel very well at all' and then still thought it was psychosomatic, so put on my backpack and walked off into the Glen of Nevis and I was having high fevers and rigours and vomiting . . .

And thought I am actually really really ill. And then walked all the way back and it took me a whole day to walk back, because I was so sick and then I lay in the road hoping a car would stop and carry me to hospital but they just beeped and drove round me. So I dragged myself all the way to the door of the hospital and then thought, 'What if it isn't appendicitis?' and they're like, 'Junior doctor, where d'you train? London? Tell me the ten signs of appendicitis and what if I can't remember them all and I'm wrong.' So I turned away from the door of the hospital and went and rang a friend who was a doctor, who then said, 'What the hell are you doing? Go back into the hospital.' So I was in tears by the time I arrived at the hospital, just afraid that I was wasting somebody's time. And I'd left the appendicitis so long that I had an abscess the size of a grapefruit tucked behind my peritoneum. I spent ten days in hospital on intravenous antibiotics and they said . . . there was so much infection inside me that it wouldn't have been safe to open me up.

Man with iPad How much longer?

Jonathon How the fuck do you know? Sometimes it's obvious, or we think it's obvious in retrospect once you've seen and examined them.

Nurse We've got no beds. None. Tell them to take them to another A&E.

Jonathon So if you took a hundred people turning up at hospital thinking they've got appendicitis and one has, does that mean that ninety-nine of them could have just seen their GP? Of course it doesn't.

Sirens in the distance.

Give A&E the capability to be able to deal with everybody who goes there and stop telling people not to go there.

Senior Consultant The only time in my life I'd ever cut down A&E attendances is by closing the department.

Marjorie We do have quite a lot of people that are called 'Mister Off'. (*She laughs.*) Because you'll get them with no ID. 'What is your name, sir?' 'Fuck off!'
    'Mister Off, is it alright if we call you by your first name?' (*She laughs.*) I've been hit and things and that with . . . We've got a football red-card system. They're banned from coming.

Junior Doctor I want to refer her to Dr Shipman.

Jonathon So morale is absolutely – it's below zero – partly because there's no beds. So people are just stuck in A&E – there's nowhere to send them. They can't go home, they can't go into hospital – they're just stuck in A&E.

Nurse Bed manager's on the phone.

Female Consultant Veronica Patterson?

The frail old woman looks up, it's her. The female consultant takes her by the hand and leads her out.

Let's get you looked at.

Nurse It's crazy, this idea of charging people who are drunk. That's not a job I want. Head of Financial Collection in Southampton A&E on a Saturday night! 'Excuse me, have you got your credit card?'

Jonathon Staff turnover is massive – everybody is off sick, everybody – as fast as they can employ people, they resign. It's just hideous.

An African couple appear with suitcases – she's pregnant.

Drunk Woman Oh, here we go. Just arrived from Heathrow. Oh yeah, come and have your baby here.

They take their coats off and have doctor and nurse's uniforms on underneath.
Ambulance sirens as another emergency arrives.

Porter You're far more likely to be treated by an immigrant than to pay for the treatment of one. Especially in London.

Elderly Woman (*off*) I want to go home. I want to go home.

The homeless man moans in pain.

Marjorie It is absolutely – after thirty-five years – it is . . . I have never seen it so stressed out.

The nervous woman starts crying again.

Man with iPad I know you're meant to see me within four hours.

Screams and shouts from off, we can't see.

Angry Woman (*off*) Get off me. Fuckin' get off me.

Doctor (*off*) You just need to calm down.

Angry Woman (*off*) I don't want her anywhere near me.

Arguing and fighting continues.

Marjorie The doctor will see you now.

SCENE TWO

We find three nurses – Hannah, Carl and Lisa – having a fag and coffee break.

Hannah Everybody's scared of the ward and, of losing your job . . . We all have a PIN number. And that's your, sort of, how would you describe it, that's your registration to practise . . . And everyone always says, 'God, you know, you must fill that in, you'll lose your PIN.' If you lose your PIN, you can't work as a nurse and so there's this . . . It's drilled into us from day one of nursing school that you can lose it.

Lisa Doing anything!

Hannah You lose your job. So *you* have this thing . . . 'Oh God, I've got to write this down, otherwise it was never done.'

Lisa (*overlapping*) And that's *everything* . . .

Carl Document *everything* . . .

Hannah If you didn't write it down, and that goes to *court*, you end up in court . . . And you lose your PIN . . .

23

You've lost your job. And this is the *constant underlying fear* that drives all of us! (*She laughs.*)

Carl Yeah, pretty much.

Hannah To keep your PIN! So there's like two parallels, there's being with the patient and then writing it all down and telling the story. And almost that's more important. Because that's – all the litigation and everything. You can get some nurses who do beautiful documentation, but (*whispers*) they're shit, shit nurses! Or forgot to write this down, or –

Lisa – or they can be fantastic . . . But they'll be pulled up on this, that and everything because they haven't got the perfect documentation or they forgot to tick a box somewhere, and it's just . . . absurd.

Hannah Yeah, it's probably been around, yeah, I'm guessing, what, ten, fifteen years . . . It's terrifying! It's not about the care, it's about the documentation, really . . .

Lisa Yeah, yeah . . .

Carl If you don't give someone a cup of tea no one notices. But if you don't do the paperwork you get ten emails about it.

Lisa And I think when people have been in the profession so many years, you can see how that's affected their practice, and, and people *do* lose that kind of nice, caring side that I'm sure they probably once had, but after years of that being drummed into you, some . . . I know a lot of people get lazy as well, don't they, over time and you kind just think, 'Well, I'll just, you know, do what I've got to do,' and it's all kind of just . . . tick-boxes, and it's like, well actually . . . it's a very human job, you've got to be very adaptable but you do see how it changes people. And it makes them quite bitter and horrible.

Hannah The, the level of fear doesn't equate to . . . the –

Carl (*overlapping*) – the level of stress . . . yeah.

Lisa (*overlapping*) The level of responsibility just doesn't cut it, you just think, 'I'm taking *so much* responsibility.' For all of these people, for you guys in intensive care, it's more lives, for me, in mental health it's safety . . .

Carl (*overlapping*) I think it is . . .

Lisa But I think it is . . . I think they're trying to kill themselves . . .

Hannah Yeah, absolutely!

Lisa And you're the one cutting the rope from around their neck, do you know what I mean, it's like . . . 'I don't get paid enough for this shit' . . . (*Laughs.*)

Hannah But, but we do say . . . and I use that as an excuse. And it's really bad, like, 'I don't get paid enough to do that.'

Lisa Yeah!

Hannah 'I'm not doing that.' (*Laughs.*) And it's awful, isn't it! But it's like, 'If I get myself involved in that . . .'

Carl Yeah.

Hannah 'I'll have so much more stress!'

Carl Like I always – like whenever I'm getting ready for work I always watch breakfast telly. And they always slate the NHS, basically, every single morning. And I just really get irritated about that, but. I think everyone just seems to slam it. More. Now. Than they ever did.

Hannah We're all too posh to wash, and all this stuff, which is just *actually ridiculous*. When you're hands deep in poo nearly every day! (*Laughs.*)

Lisa I think we actually get from people generally, like, when you're out and about, that it's quite good – like if you go out, and you're in a bar or something, and they're like, 'Oh, what do you do?' and you're like, 'Oh, I'm a nurse,' they're like, 'Oh, wow!' Like, you get quite a positive response but yeah, the media just – slates us. But, you know, I think it's very easy to slate as a profession, cos it's like – well, actually, you're not looking at the fact that we don't have *time* –

Carl Yeah . . .

Lisa – to do all that stuff, you're just saying, 'Well, nurses don't do it! They're selfish, they're lazy, they don't care,' it's much *easier* to do that than to say, 'Well, actually they don't have time, we need to employ more staff,' cos then they have to put money into it!

Carl It just seems like every year there's loads more people training to be nurses but I'm not sure where they're going. Like, if they're just quitting, or – or what.

Hannah Most people leave within about five years.

Carl Yeah.

Hannah I don't know how I can do it, physically I, I could, I don't know how I could do it in my – I come home, collapse, often have a little cry. And I think – I can't do this for – ten, twenty – I can't do this till I . . .

Lisa Like, for me, it's like – we have to restrain people . . . and it's like, that's fine now, but to be honest . . . anyone that's trying to fight you and punch you and kick you, and it's like, you can't do that for ever.

Hannah You know, it was a good day if someone said they won't kill you, if someone just threatened to kill you and they didn't *actually* try and hurt you, that was a pretty good day!

They put out their fags, knock back their drinks and head back to the ward.

SCENE THREE

A GP's surgery. Louise, a Scottish GP, is busy seeing patients, reading notes, writing out prescriptions, making phone calls – almost all at once . . .

Louise It's lovely being a GP! I had this recently from an eighty-five-year-old woman who's got – she's quite a heavy smoker and she's got quite bad lung disease – we call it COPD. So I just said to her, 'Oh you know, it's not too late to stop – stop smoking.' She's like, 'I'll never stop!' She's like, 'I've been smoking since I was eleven!' She said, 'Do you know who started me? A *doctor*!'

Jonathon appears, removing his bike helmet and reflective gear.

Cos the story is that when the doodlebugs were bombing London – she got really into this . . . terrified, sort of nervous state, and her mum took her to the doctor to see if there was anything the doctor could recommend to calm her nerves, and the doctor recommended a cigarette!

Jonathon starts working – seeing patients, writing out prescriptions, making phone calls . . .

Jonathon Some days it's like you are fighting all day with people who want things you cannot give them.

Louise There's an awful lot of, I must say, wants not needs being catered for. You know, you do see people come and they've got a one-day history of a cough and a runny nose, you know.

Jonathon Around here the patients don't have very good literacy so you can't give them written information. It's so difficult to have a . . . to have anything other than a very basic conversation.

Louise He says, 'I'm ill.' And you say, I say, 'Well, what do you think this is?' 'I don't know.' 'You don't know what this is? You don't know that when you cough, your nose is runny, you feel a bit rubbish . . . (*She laughs.*) You don't, have you ever had a cold, a cold?' It seems to me that that this folk knowledge about common everyday problems . . . has been lost in our culture.

Jonathon They have a lot of street knowledge as it were, but not knowledge you would assume people have about how their bodies work or how medicines work . . . lots of people who can barely read and write . . .

Louise There's a disconnect. I think people don't have the same family support around to say, 'Oh yeah, that's just a cold, take this hot lemon drink or whatever.' Or it's because of health anxiety I think has been stoked a lot by the media, you know. 'I went to the doctor and he said it was just a cough. It turned out to be cancer.' Everybody thinks a minor illness, they interpret it, they Google it and they say, you know . . .

Jonathon We know that with prescribed medicine, 30 per cent are never taken and 30 per cent are taken very irregularly and 30 per cent taken sufficiently to do what they're supposed to do.

Louise So I'm not wanting to be too hard-and-fast on this, I just think there has been a shift in the last two decades towards people being much less resilient.

Jonathon So much of the time you are scratching your head at the end of the morning and thinking, why did these people come in?

Louise People are affronted by the fact that they're ill. Be ill and allow yourself to be ill. This is a process. It will take as long as it takes.

Jonathon People are sometimes quite explicit about it: 'Look, Doc, I just really need to come and see you every couple of weeks to just check in, just to keep myself sane,' and other people say, 'I only go out of my flat every six weeks and that's to come here.'

Louise The main problem is there are people with real problems, real conditions, real needs and it's harder and harder to meet those simply because of just the constraints on resources and your time.

Jonathon But what you find around here is you have multiple roles which cannot be clearly distinguished.

Louise And you take the time to see people, then you end up with four-hour surgeries that are exhausting, you know, if you have longer consultations.

Jonathon So your role as friend, comforter, confidante, witness, priest, neighbour, uncle, brother, whatever, some . . . all of these is . . . sometimes you have to take on several of these roles in one consultation.

Louise Or you think, 'Well, okay, I can't cope with that, I'll just see fewer patients but each of them I'll give them more time,' then you're not offering enough appointments, people can't get an appointment, they get upset . . . So it's . . . we're struggling to provide a good service.

More patients arrive, the phones ring – it doesn't stop.

SCENE FOUR

Dave, a Brighton paramedic, at his ambulance. Getting ready to go out on a shift – putting his uniform on, getting his equipment ready.

Dave Yeah, stupid calls. Get out on the driveway, start driving down, and then you'd get on the screen . . . And this is the God's honest truth – man wants a lift to see his prostitute in, in Littlehampton! And you say to them, have you read the notes? Even people have phoned up 999 because they can't get through to *X Factor* to cast their vote . . .

Marjorie is pushing the old frail woman in a wheelchair.

Marjorie I mean, if I had my youth over again, to be quite honest, man, I'd quite like to perhaps be in the International Red Cross, and be out in the field. You know? Because it's that coping with whatever's happening. And having to respond and quickly applying . . . I like . . . it sharpens your thinking. To what's going on and that. You know?

She heads off with the frail old lady.

Dave I worked from the age of seventeen till twenty-three, in Sainsbury's. I went for a training management interview, didn't get it. And then they started putting me on tills and stuff like that, and I thought, aah I can't do this, so I left . . . To become a porter, then was a healthcare assistant on a hospital ward and then done patient transport, and then worked my way up from there, really . . . So . . . I don't like the term 'started at the bottom', but, but everyone's the same, in the NHS . . . There is a, there is a, there is a little bit of a class system, if I'm truthful, but, everyone plays their part . . . When I went from a porter to a healthcare assistant, some people wouldn't say hello to me as a porter, but then two or three weeks later when I was a healthcare assistant they'd say hello to me and I'd think that's a – just because I've changed costumes . . . You'd say hello to me . . .

I think you become not desensitised . . . but you become, you get used to . . . So . . . fingers hanging off, bones poking through legs . . . Look a bit like something out of a horror film. Emotions, that we've had – I had to walk out . . . otherwise I– I was on the verge of . . .

And even in the ambulance a, a, a three-month-old baby that was sat in one of those rocking chairs or bouncy chairs . . . That Mum had fed, Mum went away and sorted the other two children out . . . It aspirated . . . (*Drops his voice very slightly.*) Which meant the food went down on to its lungs . . . The baby was dead when we got there, but, had to hang it upside down so the milk's coming out . . . Get to A&E . . . and it's the family, screaming, that gets – it's the – people . . . that are still there, and hearing screams . . .

Mental health is one that I feel, not that I feel let down personally, but I think we let those people down because we go to them . . . As we know, mental hospitals have been closed for the care in the community side of things . . . The hospital where I am has been turned into a nice, flash, housing estate . . . All I do, as many have here, and we haven't invested, any of that . . . All I do, when I go out to them, and they're feeling suicidal, is offer them A&E, where they can go and sit in a room for four hours, waiting for the, a psychiatric nurse . . . So we're letting these, for me personally as a society, we're letting these type of people down, just because we don't invest, and we all go, we all say that, dunno when it's going to be us, ourselves, it doesn't take a lot, it doesn't take a lot . . .

I think people only speak out when it's to do with them . . . Personally, I think even, three months ago, I organised something because our pay's being, attacked, or *was* being attacked, about three months ago, because we've got to save money, allegedly. And I organised meetings three months ago, and nobody turned up. These people, even that were on the Ambulance Station, 'You not staying for the meeting?' This was on a Friday, end of my week. 'Oh I can't stay . . .' 'Where's your letter?' 'Oh it's in the recycling bin.' Then, month later, they start taking the pay away. 'Oh, what about, what about?' 'Well, I've just . . .' Do you know what I mean? So apathy does . . . Unless it affects them personally . . .

> *Four staff pass through with musical instruments*
> *under their arms – two violins, a viola and a cello.*
> *Dave takes a deep breath and heads off for his shift.*

SCENE FIVE

We meet a cardiologist. As he talks to us the actor –
helped by other actors – changes costume and make-up
and transforms in front of us.

Cardiologist Healthcare is part of the entertainment industry.

Wasn't it Voltaire who said, 'The art of medicine consists of amusing the patient while nature cures the disease.'

For hundreds of years – for most of the time medicine existed – doctors really had very few things they could actually usefully do with their patients. And yet everybody went to see their doctor. And a successful doctor was a doctor who made a patient leave happier than when they came.

In the entertainment industry, obviously, lots of things the government does, in terms of health care is just window-dressing. Like for example, Cameron's war on dementia. Making – having everybody tested for dementia, screening for dementia, which is utter nonsense. Because we haven't got any good treatments for dementia and screening patients for dementia for no good reason, well it just means you might give them the bad news earlier or unnecessarily worry them.

I would assume that perhaps some relative of Cameron went demented, so he decided, 'Well it's a problem that needs to be given more attention.' Early diagnosis is utter nonsense anyway because dementia is defined by a decline over time.

If you get acutely, suddenly sick, anything which happens fast, it's potentially relatively fixable.

So if you come in with an MI, if one of your coronaries is blocked off, you can thrombolise the patient or you can do a primary angioplasty, where you bore open the artery and stick in a stent. That cures the thing.

The interesting thing, to talk about the entertainment industry – well the first treatment for MIs was thrombolysis. Streptokinase. Clot-busting drugs.

Streptokinase is fifty pounds.

Then TPA came on the market, which is a clot-busting drug where a bit of genetically-modified bacteria is being produced. And that costs five hundred pounds.

Big, big big studies, all sorts of people saying how TPA must be better.

Possibly works slightly faster but in the end it's no better and yet there's a shift from the cheap Streptokinase to the expensive TPA. So from fifty to, to five hundred pounds. Ten times.

People then came up with angioplasties as an intervention. As a cardiologist, you like doing things with cath needles and sticking pieces of metal into patients: it's quite sexy and exciting!

So again, big studies comparing . . . And again, no difference. Angioplasty not any superior to TPA. Possibly you get a little bit less angina, you get the patients out earlier, but you do not live longer for it. It's just more hi-tech.

So we've gone up from fifty pounds to five hundred to nearly five thousand pounds, outcome exactly the same. But it keeps a lot of cardiologists ungainfully employed . . .

There is a lot of totally magical ideas about what we can achieve. Yes, there are things we can treat – things we can treat well, but lots of things we can't treat . . . The ravages of old age, we can't treat. Most cancers, yes we can treat a little bit for exorbitant amounts of money. Most chronic illnesses we can palliate, but we can't cure. Yet people have got this idea – everything is fixable, curable . . . And we can sort of promise immortality and eternal health.

And they are magical beliefs and – it's a bit like a religious belief, and obviously as doctors we perpetuate this myth because we pretend we are sort of all-curing, all-knowing and we can achieve miracles.

We do so many things really to entertain the patients or ourselves without adding an awful lot of value.

SCENE SIX

A finance department of a hospital. Accountants – in visors like old fashioned bank tellers – are frantically working away at calculators and computers. Costs of treatments are spewing out on a loop in the background throughout. The accountants talk over this.

Ten-minute GP appointment £37

Accountant 1 Our healthcare system is, value for money, the cheapest in the world, in terms of what you get from it.

A pair of crutches £9.50

Accountant 1 We get outcomes better than Americans, and we pay half the amount of money for it.

Tonsil removal procedure £1,044

Accountant 2 Because our population grows, ages – we've got more chronic disease . . .

34

Hospital food per person per day £8.77

Accountant 1 The biggest reason I think for rising costs tends to be healthcare technology. Not the demographic time bomb but healthcare technology . . .

An ambulance call-out £218

Accountant 1 All these kind of widgets which have been sold by some scamster, knocking on the Department of Health's door saying you can save loads of money but it never does.

Total cost of tonsil removal operations in one year £51 million

Accountant 2 Most of the costs of the NHS are paying people, and pay costs continue to rise . . .

One missed hospital appointment £108

Accountant 2 Pressures on the NHS budget grow by about 4 per cent a year over and above inflation.

Total cost of missed GP appointments per year £162 million

Accountant 1 GDP – typically, so our national wealth grows at just over 2 per cent a year on average.

Intensive care bed per day £1,932

Accountant 2 So health is taking a bigger, bigger and bigger share of the pie.

Appendix removal £2,300

Accountant 2 So people say, 'Ah yeah but the health service can become more productive, or the rest of the economy becomes more productive . . .'

Tonsillectomy £985

Accountant 2 The best estimates are that it can get about, more productive by about one and a half per cent a year.

Caesarean delivery £1,143.50

Accountant 1 So, to reach 4 per cent, that leaves about two and half per cent a year on top of inflation that we need to grow the NHS budget by.

Appendectomy £1,247

Accountant 2 And we over the last four or five years, we've grown the budget by about 1 per cent a year more than inflation.

Amputation of toe £901.50

Accountant 1 Hence there's a gap. And that won't ever go away.

Patient–GP contact cost per minute £3.90

Accountant 2 There is no country in the developed world over the post-war period that has managed to avoid spending more over the long term.

Elective inpatient £3,375

Accountant 2 If you introduce charging, the research and all the evidence shows that it increases the amount of healthcare that you consume.

Outpatient attendance £111

Accountant 1 The very people who need it become less likely to use it.

Diabetes to NHS per hour £1.5 million

Accountant 2 So you get the middle-class well, who start using it more, and the poorer people who need it more, use it less.

Cataract operation £900 per eye

Accountant 1 What's the most cost-effective treatment?

Vasectomy £250

Accountant 2 One way you measure cost-effectiveness is in QALYs, which is a quality-adjusted life year.

Stroke patient daycare facilities £208

Accountant 2 The QALY is based on the number of years of life that would be added by the intervention.

One hip replacement operation £5,459

Accountant 1 How many pounds do you have to spend to give somebody an extra year of quality life?

Prescription costs per GP consultation £43.90

Accountant 1 We have a committee of people who look at the evidence and come up with a number, and basically say – 'The NHS can afford, roughly at the moment, somewhere between £20,000 to £40,000 to keep you alive for a year . . .'

One night in hospital £225

Accountant 2 'If it costs more than that, we're not paying. You're on your own. If you've got £40,000, you can do it yourself, but otherwise, too bad.'

Total NHS spend on arthritis per year £560 million

Accountant 1 If you're going to stop doing stuff, which do you choose? 'Keep looking after dementia patients at home or stop doing fertility treatment?'

Total cost of laxatives to NHS per year £60 million

Accountant 1 For a course of IVF, you could keep a dementia patient going at home for a couple of years.

Ambulance emergency calls £7

Accountant 1 Looking after a dementia patient at home, who's falling over and incontinent – I think that's actually more important than fertility treatment for people who are forty-five years old and never got round to it earlier.

Cost of negligence claims against NHS per year £1.6 billion

Accountant 2 Harsh.

A&E attendance £124

They get their heads down and carry on number crunching as costs continue to spew out.

Circumcision £931.50

End-of-life care / cancer diagnosis £11,268

Dementia diagnosis £17,231

Alcoholism £10,431

Diabetes complications £12,979

SCENE SEVEN

Dr Malhotra, a busy cardiologist, appears. A nurse passes by eating a Mars bar.

Dr Malhotra I would say easily two-thirds of what comes to the NHS, both in primary care and secondary care, is related to lifestyle-related illness. 80 per cent of cardiovascular disease, and cardiovascular disease is the biggest killer in the Western world, is lifestyle-related. So specifically poor diet, lack of activity, smoking, alcohol. Though poor diet is responsible for more disease than physical inactivity, smoking and alcohol combined. Food can be the most powerful form of medicine but also the slowest form of poison.

I'm an interventional cardiologist, putting stents in people . . .

A stressed-looking doctor passes and takes out his cigarettes, he's heading out for a break.

So we need to reduce the availability of junk food and sugar, like we do with tobacco.

When the public smoking ban was brought in, in Scotland there was a 17 per cent decrease in hospital admissions for heart attack within six months.

60 per cent of the UK population is either overweight or obese, one in three children by the time they leave primary school are also in the same category, and the trends are suggesting this is going to get a lot worse by 2050, that 60 per cent figure will become 90 per cent.

Ultimately, the obesity problem is rooted in the food environment. Choice has been limited because you can't avoid processed food. Even hospitals have junk food onsite. Schools. Gyms.

Most doctors know nothing about nutrition and in fact I know studies that show that most doctor's understanding of nutrition comes from TV and magazines.

So I used to drink, for example, I calculated I spent about £7,000 over a space of around ten years on Lucozade. I go to the gym regularly, I believe in physical activity as being important for health and I love doing it, I run, I go to the gym, and it's every day. I used to have one of these every day thinking I needed this for my . . . And then a study comes out showing that all of the initial studies suggesting it was good for hydration was basically industry-sponsored, very weak.

The *British Medical Journal* did a big study on this and they said, 'This is absolute nonsense, you know, it doesn't enhance, it's not necessary . . . You just drink water.' And I was thinking, 'Wow, I was drinking all this sugar, I don't need it.' Switched to water instead of sugary drinks, still do the same exercise routines.

*Dr Malhotra stops at a large vending machine which is
full of fatty snacks and sugary food and drinks.*

Doctors don't always know best and we're also subject to
the same environmental pressures – 50 per cent of NHS
employees are now overweight or obese. You'd think we
are the ones that should know better.

*Dr Malhotra puts in some change, presses the buttons
to choose an apple and eats it.*

If you eat an apple a day, there's some good evidence to
say that's just as effective as statins at preventing a heart
attack.

Government ministers in one year had had over eighty
meetings in relation to obesity with people who were
food industry representatives, and not a single meeting
with a doctor or a public advocate.

In medical school, there was not a single lecture on
impact of nutrition on health, not a single lecture. We are
conditioned to treat people with drugs. Diagnose and
treat. Diagnose and treat. Diagnose and treat.

Dr Malhotra rushes off to see the next patient.

SCENE EIGHT

*Surgery. We find two surgeons mid-operation – they're
the Ex-NHS Chief Exec and an Ex-Department of
Health National Director. They're assisted by nurses and
anaesthetists as they operate on the patient – the frail old
woman. There is a large opening in her stomach.*

Ex-NHS Chief Exec When a government comes under
pressure about something, they think that reorganising
the NHS is a cost-free thing. And so you come in and
reorganise, and it gives a semblance that something is
being done.

A Secretary of State – I won't tell you which one – he said, 'We need to give people the idea that the NHS is being renewed, right.' And somebody came up with the idea that when you smell fresh paint you think something has been made new, you know.

So he came up with the idea of repainting the whole of the NHS. Right, that every ward, every hospital would be repainted. And this would be a big signal to the whole population. You know, there are thousands and thousands of wards across . . . The idea of disrupting . . . I mean, you just can't imagine.

But we had a real struggle . . . to make it not happen. We managed to get the Business Secretary to say, if you bought the amount of paint, it would so distort the paint market . . . it would . . . that it would be dead.

Ex-Department of Health National Director So I, I got to work with four or five different kind of Secretaries of State and Prime Ministers, Labour and Tory: Blair, Brown, Lansley . . . Hunt, a little bit. Burnham.

Ex-NHS Chief Exec This time of the electoral cycle, so this time last time . . . The Opposition politicians get access to people like me, to talk to them about . . . 'cause we have to get ready in case they win the election, to create their whatsit.

Ex-Department of Health National Director So first of all, they were all very committed. It wasn't very obvious what their politics was, actually.

Ex-NHS Chief Exec Cameron has . . . well, you know, my dealings with Cameron is, essentially, he wants it all to go away. Sorry, he doesn't want the NHS to be destroyed . . . He just thinks there's nothing in it for him, and politically there's nothing in it for him. Most politicians are not really interested in healthcare.

Ex-Department of Health National Director 'How can I make this better? You know, I want to make it better, and I've got Parliament and the media on my back. Tell me how it is that I can reduce death rates or improve patient experience.' But the only thing they can really control is structure. So they start off wanting to figure out how to reach out, so that when Missus Miggins arrives in A&E, she'll get – in Kettering – she'll get a caring experience, and they can't. And they kind of figure out within six months that the only thing they can really do is control the structure. And . . . 'Not everything's right so the structure must be wrong so I'll change the structure.' They're all told not to do it. And they do it.

Ex-NHS Chief Exec It's not really a job that gets you on in politics, so it's not . . . If I want to be the Prime Minister, do I want to be the Secretary of State for Health? No, you want to be the Foreign Secretary, or Home Secretary, you know, or the Chancellor – that's where the big jobs are. It's not seen as a big job. In Whitehall, it's described as the biggest train set.

They spend, sort of, a few months learning what the job is. They then work out what they want to do. And then they have about six months to nine months to do it, before they're reshuffled somewhere else.

They continue with the operation.

End of Act One

Tea Break

Maternity Ward. We enter just after a new baby has been born. Exhausted mother, emotional father, tiny real baby, mess everywhere. A nurse cleans them and pulls a curtain round. Marjorie offers us a cup of tea from a tea trolley, a large tea urn and old fashioned green cups and saucers. She talks to us as she hands out the tea.

Marjorie I've always been into the full, rounded support of a person.

And I took a pride. I could get nice normal deliveries. I loved me standing deliveries. It means I'm cross-legged on the floor, catching this babe, but we get a good, good delivery. No stitches. Very rare I have to stitch my ladies. Got a little trick. I like my water births, but equally I'm a nurse as well, so could give support in high-dependency area, and also scrub for sections. Which I quite enjoyed. I would say, over the last sort of six, seven years, it's becoming tense. And certainly around obstetrics.

I lost two babies before I had my girls. And I nearly died myself actually with the post-partum haemorrhage after the boy that I lost. (*Beat.*) But you knew, you had a lot of respect for nature. And of course basically I've been brought up north; we're round the farming stock and things. It is amazing, but you know that nature does thin things out. And there is a biological law and order, isn't there, of, of the strong will survive and the weak will fall by the side. And really what we're doing is supporting the weak, and strengthening them, isn't it?

Survival and that. But there has to be a realism. And so much so there was a realism that I remember when I was having the children, we used to get that £25 maternity grant, and believe you me, you used to be, you'd be able to get a pram and a cot for that. Now you're lucky if you get a spoke on a wheel in a pram.

You'd go choose your pram and your cot, but the store would not send that to you until they knew you had been safely delivered. There was like a sense of knowing that, you know, sometimes babies made it, sometimes babies didn't.

Yeah? It was just the way of things.

We have to look at the whole thing of death and dying, don't you? Life is: being born and passing through, isn't it? You know? (*She laughs.*) You've got to enjoy what you can in between and things, and that. But sometimes perhaps people do have unrealistic expectations, don't they? And there are times when we are incredibly challenged.

And we have often seen it in oncology where you've got young teenagers and young men and women that are having to face the . . . that they are going to die . . .

And then it seems quite bizarre when you've got like, somebody like 103 coming in the other day, you know, and it's their daughter that's panicky because she's vomiting and things, but, you know, but, really she shouldn't be on her trolley in the hospital, she should be all comfortable at home . . .

There've been 101-year-olds with a pacemaker put in, you know? You've got to think, haven't you? You've got to rationalise things. It's not that we're putting anybody on the dumping ground. But, you know, there has to be a sense of realism, hasn't there?

But what, what we're missing is the good old-fashioned, the community, where you had, you had your district nurse, didn't you, who was a midwife and nurse.

She was the sage femme, she was the woman in the community, or the man, obviously we've got to . . . that knew what to do when so and so were labouring, or so and so . . . 'Oh, she's been labouring too long. This baby should have come now. Will you get so-and-so to come and help out?' Or, 'Oh, he's dying,' you know? And things, whatever. 'What are we going to do?' And things like that. You'd get to know that person, wouldn't you?

To help out. A majority of things would have been supported in the home.

And of course the GPs would come out. You can't get them out now, can you?

And that. And I can remember as a kid when I had all the, you know, you had the chickenpox and measles . . . Whenever the GP came through the door, just hearing him come through the door. Ah. (*She sighs.*) It made you feel better. Do you know what I mean? And it felt like part of the family.

Act Two: Diagnosis

A large hospital ward with beds. Some beds curtained off – mini set pieces to be revealed behind them.
   Nurses and doctors pass through.
   A nurse passes by with a viola.
   Paul, an ex-Department of Health advisor, appears.

Paul I'm the same age as the National Health Service.

Jonathon appears. He introduces people.

Jonathon This is Paul, ex-Department of Health advisor.

Paul I was born in April 1948, and it was born in July, so I really did have a mum who would say to me, from the age of when I could remember, that I was really lucky, because when we went to the doctor we didn't have to pay, and that when my brother, who was six years older than me, went to the doctor, they always kept a half crown on the mantelpiece.

Jacky, a radiologist, appears.

Jacky I went to speak up in Liverpool last year . . .

Jonathon Jacky, radiologist.

Jacky And somebody said: 'I remember that my younger brother was ill and we all sat, my mother and father sat around the table and counted the money and sent little Billy down the road to get the doctor, and while they were making all these decisions and all the rest of it, the child died and then somebody was then sent running to get Billy to get him back again before he got to the doctor and lost his money,' but even in the middle of all this tragedy of the child dying, it was: 'Let's have our money back,' and it's very . . .

The ex-NHS Chief Exec appears.

Ex-NHS Chief Exec When it was set up, the original documentation didn't say, 'Better Health', or 'Health Services for the People', or whatever.

Jonathon He's the ex-NHS Chief Executive.

Ex-NHS Chief Exec It was called 'In Place of Fear'. Which is the big thing.

Paul And so I'm of a generation where the transformation took place, and my mum went on about it through the whole of her life.

Jacky Our oldest son lives in New York, and he has been significantly ill on a couple of occasions recently, and he didn't get insurance and we asked him to, and he had to walk into an A&E department and be asked, 'I want 800 dollars before I'll even look at you,' when he couldn't walk actually because he'd dislocated something, is just to understand what it's like for people over there.

Ex-NHS Chief Exec I was diagnosed two years ago with Type II Diabetes, and you . . . the thing . . . alright, you've got fear, 'cause you think, what's gonna happen to me? But what you haven't got is the fear that most of the rest of the world have, which is, am I gonna have to sell my house, am I gonna go bankrupt, how am I gonna be able to pay bills, all of those sort of things.

Jonathon Like one way – because it's worth whatever – 9 per cent of GDP – one way of just imagining it is like every eleventh hour that you work goes towards looking after people. No matter how shit your job and how much you hate it, you think – like at the end of the day – like this hour is going to be keeping somebody alive on intensive care, it's going to be giving chemotherapy to somebody with cancer, it's going to be helping somebody with depression have a course of counselling therapy. And that's nice. That's a nice feeling, yeah.

Ex-NHS Chief Exec Doesn't every generation have to relearn the reason why we did it?

A nurse appears, all starched and in white, almost like an angel. A choir sings. Are we in a hospital or a church?
The NHS Regulator appears.

NHS Regulator Is our love of the NHS its biggest problem?

In other words, is our emotional attachment to the NHS gonna stop it changing in the way that it needs to, to continue to thrive and survive?

But in a way it's, you know, it's what's great about it and what's really sort of quite scary about it, because if you, if you hold it, if you put the thing on an altar, you're not gonna want to change it, and it's got to change.

So is this sentimentality gonna get in the way of its long-term success? That would be the question for me.

Jonathon That's the NHS Regulator.

We glimpse patients and family members on the ward.
Julie Bailey at the end of a hospital bed. The frail old woman is asleep in the bed next to her.

Julie She had a hiatus hernia – had it all through the summer, and she was a bugger, my mum was, for fried tomatoes and kidney. Anyway, I did the fried tomatoes, and of course, that upset the hernia, didn't it? So anyway, they took her in . . .

Marjorie sits on the edge of a bed in a gown tied at the back ready for her operation.

48

Marjorie I had an experience of being a patient, it's quite fun.

Peter Bamford stands next to a bed where his young baby son sleeps.

Peter We've had lots of sleepless nights because . . . just terrifying . . . when your baby's not certain to get through the night, y' know . . .

Julie Bailey sits down on a chair next to the bed.

Julie My mum was on oxygen – she'd been a long-term smoker. She had respiratory problems for a long time, but we managed them well between us. She was 86. She wasn't a well woman, don't get me wrong, and she probably wouldn't have lived very much longer, but she shouldn't have died the way she did and when she did.

Pause.

My niece found her collapsed in a chair without her oxygen. She asked the porter, 'Get the oxygen' . . . They kept telling her that there were people iller than my mum that they were having to deal with – and there probably were. But anyway, eventually, my niece rang me and she said, 'Get up here – we're about to lose Nan.' So I went running up the stairs, pressed the red alarm bell and just started screaming on the ward. And three or four doctors came, put Mum into the bed and pulled the curtains around, worked on her, and that was it – they revived her.

So from that moment on, I said I wasn't going to leave Mum – they'd left her to die, basically. With limited resources, they had to prioritise and the elderly weren't the priority. But I stayed there then for eight weeks.

It was horrendous, absolutely horrendous, because the first six weeks, you see, we could help the other patients, because they were all infirm – Mum was the fittest, in the

49

end. She was helping other people! But the last two weeks – dreadful.

I'd say 40 per cent of the staff were just absolute angels, they just ran themselves ragged – but 60 per cent of the staff, they just bullied the patients, they bullied other staff.

So some days, they'd come, and they'd come to the door and tell you that they'd lost the drug keys – you couldn't have drugs that day.

I never saw the managers. I spoke to the matron, the first time I complained, and she said, 'Oh it's a blip in services' – that's a common thing. They'd push staff in for the first few days, but then they couldn't maintain it. I don't know if you know, but there was something like – I think it was 360 nurses short at Mid Staffs.

The Government directive was, that all hospitals had to be foundation trust hospitals within a certain period. So all these young, aspiring managers, chief execs wanted to be FTs, because it was seen as the done thing, you see, because they can – you can lend money. They could raise their own money, independent from the Department of Health, and they can get loans.

You had to have a surplus of something like £10 million to go through for FT. So what Martin Yeates did was, he slashed the nurses, the workforce. It's always the workforce, the front line that gets slashed, isn't it?

She gets up from her chair and comes into the ward.

There was always a confused man, there was always a confused man. You'd wake up in the middle of the night, and you'd be like that – somebody would be over you. You always had more confused patients coming in of a weekend – one of the kinder staff told me that very often they were either coming off drugs or alcohol, so they became more aggressive at the weekend. So this Thursday, we had this guy – he was just really confused and he kept grabbing the woman opposite's bag and she was immobile, couldn't do anything. And he just kept coming and coming. Anyway, she grabbed the bag and fell out of the bed. So as I ran over to get her off the floor, he ran over to my mum, grabbed her out and grabbed – well, Mum died with the black marks all over her – saying it was his bed.

I saw the sister. I said, 'I've had enough – I'm making a complaint.' And she begged me, she says. 'Please don't make a complaint – you'll just get us into trouble.' And I says – 'Well, what can I do? He's just . . . Because there was just nobody to help you.'

So I wrote a letter to the Chief Exec, 'That's it – it'll be better now, Mum.'

Took it up to his office, put it through the door – and about two o'clock that morning – I always went to the toilet – ran down the corridor and ran back – I couldn't get down the corridor without people shouting you – 'Help! Help! Help! Help!' So I ran back to Mum, and the bloody staff had removed my chair.

The chair next to the bed is gone.

That was it then – they just turned against me. I cried – for the first time there, I just stood and just sobbed. It was like a real defining moment, that was. I thought – 'Christ, what have they – what are they capable of?' Because there was no other chair – they'd taken them all. So they'd ran down – so it's like these hardworking staff who haven't got time to get to the patients . . .

Allyson, professor of public health research and policy, passes through.

Allyson So what they did in 1990 was they created a market, an internal market. Services were now set up like little firms.

Jonathon reappears.

Jonathon This is Allyson, professor of public health research and policy.

Allyson Then they created these foundation trusts, which were given more and more powers to raise their own money and also to make surpluses for the first time.

In the old days, if you were making big profits, it meant that actually you were probably doing something wrong.

If you made a profit at the end of the year, it would all come back to the centre of the region and then be redistributed out again.

It wasn't romantic. The evidence is there; for fifty years it worked. And the government was able to control the cost. I mean, for the first forty or fifty years, the cost never rose above 4.5 per cent of GDP.

She passes through.
Julie reappears.

Julie The next thing . . . Mum was dying. It was the end, yeah.

She comes back to the bed. It's empty.
Pause.

When I left the ward in the early hours of the morning, Dr Karantha – they must have rang him, the consultant, he came down and came to me, and he said, 'We've never known anybody like you. You've been a fantastic daughter, you know, you've done everything you could for her.' I said, 'Yeah, I might have, but you haven't.' He says – 'What do you mean?' I said, 'You're killing these patients.' 'No – everything will be alright. Come and give me a cuddle' – all this behaviour. I just walked out. And I got home, I was in a really bad place, and I was really – I couldn't stop pacing.

So the following day, popped through my letterbox is a letter from the Director of Nursing. Commiserations – sorry I'd lost my mum and if I've got any concerns about the standard of care, give her a ring. I thought – 'Right, I'm going to give you a ring.' She said I was going through the grieving process and I was going through the anger stage – and once I'd had time to calm down, I'd make a valuable asset at the hospital, speaking about my patient experience.

The afternoon that we buried Mum, I went straight to the MP. 'These are very serious allegations that you're making.' And I said, 'Yeah, I am. Too right!' And so I thought, 'Well, he's going to do something here.' I got this letter back basically saying . . . everything's fine at the hospital.

So I put a letter to the local newspaper and within hours they did a front-page spread. Practically overnight, I had about forty people come forward, all telling me the same thing. But it's at that point that I realised – because I'm just thinking this is Ward 11, you see – no idea this is anywhere else in the hospital – it's at that point I realised that it's the hospital, there's lots of . . .

By this time I'm thinking – I don't think I'm well, to be honest, I'm not in a well place, but I'm out – I'm out every day and every night delivering leaflets.

Anyway, I contacted the Healthcare Commission. 'We've been in overnight and we found every one of your – There were 66 things that I could prove that we'd all seen. We've seen all of your . . . ' And that was the trigger that made them launch the Healthcare Commission investigation, which lasted nearly twelve months.

But in the meantime, as they launched their investigation, the hospital were awarded foundation trust status. They were now a flagship hospital.

Martina (hospital manager) and Tony (orthopaedic consultant) pass through.

Tony It could have happened anywhere –

Jonathon Here's Martina, hospital manager, and Tony, orthopaedic consultant.

Tony – because every hospital across the country was under tremendous financial pressure.

Martina Financial pressure, absolutely.

Tony Because when the financial crisis hit and you're in recession, everyone's got to cut back.

The ex-NHS Chief Exec appears.

Ex-NHS Chief Exec I think the reality is that healthcare is quite a dangerous thing. We harm about 10 per cent of the people that we treat.

Tony There was a huge drive that you will be really in danger if you don't, you know, become an FT. That all seems to have gone quiet and it's all about patient safety at the minute. It really is.

Ex-NHS Chief Exec And that can be anything from 'we give them the wrong drug' right the way through to 'we cut off the wrong limb'. And so that's . . . but I don't think the public understand that.

Martina There's a huge drive at the moment to meet the target before . . . obviously before the election, so all this extra funds have been put in and all these extra people are being brought in to meet this target . . .

Ex-NHS Chief Exec See, those of us who work in the business have always known it. But as it becomes more transparent, more and more people are gonna know this.

They pass through.
Julie reappears.

Julie The day the Healthcare Commission report came out, the press were just everywhere – it was on the TV headline news. But that night that I went home to over three hundred emails, telling me that this was a national problem – it was all over the country. So that's when we started our campaign for the public inquiry.

So what the Tories did then – it was the election – it's the same – I mean, have you heard of the Bristol Royal Infirmary Inquiry? Ten years before – same circumstances, but it was the Labour Party who were coming. So the Tories came and courted us.

Cameron came to the café and he said, 'If we get elected, we'll give you the public inquiry and examine the whole of the NHS.' So with that, I put a piece of paper in front of him, and said, 'Sign this.' And he signed it, on camera.

So we got – as soon as they got elected, we got, they gave us the public inquiry and we were core participants, and what we were able to do was give our own recommendations.

It was the Department of Health we blamed for what had gone on. It wasn't the nurses, but it was things like the director of nursing, the union reps at the hospital, because they weren't supporting the staff that were speaking out.

Well, the conclusion – the Francis Report – we ended up with 290 recommendations.

There wasn't one person that was held to account for the failings at Mid Staffs. And one of the recommendations was – it would be a criminal offence to silence a whistleblower within the NHS. And it hasn't been implemented, and now Robert Francis has gone back on his word.

We haven't got the mechanism where NHS staff feel safe to make a mistake.

Pause.

Andrew Lansley's reforms were bloody, absolutely – he didn't understand them himself. But that's one of the problems with the NHS that we've got now is – it's run on a five-year cycle. So there's no incentive to do anything, is there, long term? 'Let's just have a tinker.'

Ideally, we need to take politics out of the NHS.

There was this huge campaign from the community against us, a backlash. I used to get death threats and all sorts of things. They were shutting A&E overnight, because they couldn't get the consultants to work there.

It was on notices all over the town that I'd said 'Shut the hospital'! 'I hope she bloody dies in a bloody ambulance going to Stoke, because she's shut this hospital.'

That was the straw that broke the camel's back. I sold up and moved away.

She looks over to the empty hospital bed.

I still now – I mean, I've lost my mum, eight years come November – and I can still now wake in the middle of the night and I'm back on that ward.

Jacky comes on to the ward.

Jacky Labour did really turn a lot of things around . . . They were over-keen on targets, but some of the targets they put in were good, people were moved through A& E quicker, and we were underfunded compared to practically every other health service, certainly in the first world, so they put money in, and that money really really showed, the results showed, the waiting lists went down, the outcomes really started to improve very quickly . . .

We hear a rowdy House of Commons. Andrew Lansley speaks as the ward is busy with doctors and nurses going about their business.

Andrew Lansley The Health and Social Care Act has now passed into law. At the heart of the reforms are two simple principles. First, patients should have more control over the care they receive. Second, those responsible for patient care – the doctors, nurses and others who work in our NHS – should have the freedom and power to lead an NHS that delivers continually improving care for its patients. The Health and Social Care Act explicitly supports the core principles of the NHS – care provided free at the point of use, funded from general taxation, and based on need and not ability to pay. But the Act is only the beginning of a journey. My ambition is for a clinically led NHS that delivers the best possible care for patients. Politicians should not be able to tell clinicians how to do their jobs . . .

Allyson breaks through.

Allyson The Health and Social Care Act was a sort of momentous actually or devastating act because it removes the duty of the Secretary of State to secure and provide comprehensive healthcare for all.

That duty has been watered down from 'provide' to 'promote' . . . So it's not your responsibility. It's the abdication bill, which is what David Owen called it.

She takes out the tiny original act that created the NHS.

That's it. The original act. Look how thin it is compared with . . .

She takes out the large heavy Health and Social Care Act.

And that's not even the notes, remember, that's just the act. Four hundred and x pages. This is what was brought in –

She holds up the original act.

– and endured for sixty years, and this is what they had to do to destroy it.

She holds up the new act.

The government has passed more than twenty pieces of legislation to dismantle this (*original act*) and it's taken them over twenty years, but this is the final bit (*new act*), this is when you remove that duty, and the new structures that have been put in place are to ensure market provision.

NHS Regulator I don't think Andrew Lansley, the then Health Secretary, was really trying to push it, certainly not very much further, but for people who didn't like it, it was easy to characterise what he was trying to do as if he was trying to marketise or privatise the NHS . . . And those are *such* emotional words –

Jacky Cameron didn't really know or take any interest in what was going on, just thought Lansley knew what he was doing, and that Lansley had a plan, but when the coalition was formed, Oliver Letwin and Danny Alexander had to sit down and bring together the policies from the two different parties over a broad area, including over the NHS, and they came up with a whole load of bullshit which Lansley never wanted, shut Lansley out of the room and told Lansley what it was going to be, so a lot of people didn't realise that, that in fact Lansley then had to go out and sell something that hadn't been his original plan.

Ex-NHS Chief Exec I was appointed by Tony Blair. And he was much more in favour of privatisation than I find the current government. He certainly did much more about it than the current government.

I spent quite a lot of time during that period, trying to explain to Labour ministers what their own policy was, 'cause they didn't really know.

NHS Regulator If you've got a private sector organisation that can provide care which is at least as good as an NHS organisation, for exactly the same price, and can also make a bit of a profit in the process, what's the problem?

Jacky So when people keep saying as they've said from the beginning, competition is going to be really good for the NHS because the private sector, you know, they're better and cheaper and innovative, well, how do you know? All those outcomes and financial figures, you can't get them under the commercial confidentiality.

Jim So the NHS is an *act* of solidarity. It's a statement. It's the last remaining socialist statement in this country that, you know, 'from each according to their means, to each according to their need' – it's the last thing that does that.

Jonathon That's Jim, managing director of a privately owned healthcare company.

Ex-NHS Chief Exec You know, some of these private companies, like Care UK, or Virgin, or whatever, they'll spend half a million quid on a bid. The NHS bid, you tend to have to do it while you're doing everything else at the same time.

Jacky Serco won a big contract, a big community contract, I think out in East Anglia somewhere. They undercut the local NHS who bid for it by 10 million. They moved in and 'allegedly' sacked a lot of staff, then found that they couldn't deliver the service and then turned around to the local NHS and said: 'Can you lend us some doctors and some physios and some nurses?'

Jim Doctors do the weirdest things to us. They cut us open with knives and they give us poisons and it's a very deep act of trust. It's essential for us to believe that that's a very pure act. That all that's motivating it is – you know, deep values about healing. And the idea that there are other complicated things about money and politics . . . it's very corrosive, that. So I think the idea – and it, and, you know, there *is* money and there *is* politics. And there *are* interests.

Allyson The BBC should say: 'Your NHS was abolished on March the whatever 2012, and as a result, now we've got all these six-hour waits going on,' and this is what the real story is, instead of which it's: 'The NHS is failing yet again, patient six hours, patient dissatisfaction' etc., etc. . . . . But they never do, the BBC didn't report it at all.

Jacky There were so many MPs and peers who had interests in private medicine who should have never been voting about whether that should have happened.

Jim I've been a manager in the NHS for twenty-seven years. I made this big change two years ago to work for a private company that just provides NHS care.

People have taken me to one side and said, you know, 'You are *betraying* the NHS,' whereas I wake up every day thinking I still work for it. The pay cheque's signed by someone else.

Right now, I've got – I don't know, four hundred million pounds of contracts. They turn over every three years and loads of people would like us not to be involved at all, so if we don't do a good job, it's all gone.

NHS Regulator In health, in most other European countries, there's a lot more private sector provision, and they're perfectly comfortable with it, and yet here, in the one area of health there is just this enormous aversion to it.

Jim I don't see that Mid Staffs failed because it was a public organisation; it failed because its leadership lost sight of what was – what it was trying to do. Got disconnected. Could happen to us.

NHS Regulator I don't quite understand it, and indeed if you talk to people who've gone to a private sector hospital or something, for NHS care, they're generally very positive about it, and it doesn't matter to them who owns the hospital.

Jim GPs – great, fantastic colleagues: always been private companies. When the deal was done in '48 to create the health service, the GPs basically said no. Which has been forgotten, but. They did. And what Bevan did was he allowed them to carry on running their own businesses contracted to the NHS, as compared to hospital doctors who became employed by the NHS.

Jacky There is a democratic deficit, the fact that you can stand on a platform and say no top-down reorganisation and then bring in the biggest top-down reorganisation within six weeks of being elected.

Jim 'Get the politics out . . .' You can't, you can't get the politics out of a hundred-and-ten-billion pound public service.

Jacky Why aren't the public bothered? Do you think it's bread and circuses? I think to a degree people have got Sky TV and six beers so who cares?

Jim You know, the Labour Party policy, 'Let's have more of stuff,' or the Tory Party policy, 'Let's have better stuff,' and some of it . . . it just . . . none of it's particularly real and people in the service aren't . . .

I was in Number Ten and they were more or less saying, 'Yeah, we've got a policy that takes us up to the election.' So they've both got policies that are about getting into power.

We find Marjorie sitting on the edge of her hospital bed.

Marjorie I'm small stature as you can see. My grandmother was, my mother was . . . But we've had this genetic problem when we go through menopause, our breasts get – (*She mimes bigger.*)

We've always had nice figures but your back feels like it's going to rip off with the weight . . . and it was pressing on a nerve and would make me lose grip and drop things.

Then the best of it all. My husband noticed this: 'You're scaring me in the night. You're snoring but sometimes (*with a laugh*) you don't seem to be breathing . . .' (*She laughs.*) So we went through a sleep study and I'm having sleep apnoea's with massive drops in oxygen and desaturations because of the massive weight on me chest. It was literally like somebody sat on your . . . on your chest thing. The problem with that is long term it leads to heart problems and possible stroke because your body's on red alert through the night.

Pause.

So we're getting masses of information out to say really I do need this operation and I got to the point where it didn't matter if you took the whole lot off. Do a bilateral mastectomy if you want . . . but they wanted to keep some shape or form, you know? (*Beat.*) So I had to have four kilos taken off . . . (*She laughs.*) A six-hour operation.

They had to book that theatre for that day and I do feel I've taken off the NHS but equally I've paid in. My first job ever was in 1969 when I was an office junior after I left school as a teenage mum and I paid, I put a stamp on the card. You literally put a stamp on a card for the NHS.

I did in fact look at a private consultant and he took one look and he said, 'Marjorie, you are definitely an NHS case because this is not a frivolous thing.' He says, 'I will do it for them if they will free up the budget to pay me to do it for you.' He says, 'I will get you through but,' he says, 'this is a dangerous operation,' which it is, because of the large masses that you're taking off and thing . . .

Pause.

Well, I goes through that.

Beat.

And the wounds did break down cos they filled up with tissue fluid and the wounds (*she makes an exploding noise*) blew. I had a wound here that I could to second knuckle deep to pack. They repositioned nipples, it's just a fancy malarkey they're not nipples like they used to be. This one didn't take and that one dropped off, it became necrotic. It had, it looked like something out of an African tribal thing. I had a cavity that went right the way through here (*she points to her right breast*), communicated here and then a fissure around here.

She wells up and starts silently crying. Long pause.

(*Through tears.*) And I got told . . . (*voice breaking*) I couldn't have a district nurse . . . and I got told I couldn't have the dressings that I needed . . . (*Long pause.*) And I was costing too much.

Marjorie breathes in. Long pause. She fills up again.

I'm sorry. I can't bear this.

She breathes in trying to get herself together.

(*Voice breaking.*) What kind of budget management makes people feel that they are unworthy of being looked after? Eh?

My surgeon was good, don't get me wrong and I told him, you know I'm a scrub nurse I've done surgery and things . . . and really everyone that submits to an operation and no matter how good a surgeon is you're always at the mercy of how the anatomy's going to react to it.

I says, 'I'm just so grateful to get rid of the weight off my back. You've enabled me to breathe again. That's the main thing.

'So I'm not going to litigate,' and he got ever so upset and frustrated with the fact that the nursing side and GP side of things were going budget, budget, budget.

And I cried with him as well, because we're of old school, we've come from same training, from the same . . . 'What's happening to health service when . . . We never denied folk, did we? Denied folk.'

And the one thing that happened. I had necrosis, so there's nothing worse than the smell of rotting flesh. And there's nothing worse when it's your rotting flesh that you're smelling . . .

It stunk and, you know, when I look after patients with manky smelly wounds and things, to give them some dignity back, it's just the simple things. You just put a charcoal dressing on and I got told by my GP that, 'We can't supply that. We've had a directive not to prescribe unnecessary dressings.' I says, 'You're telling me this while I am sat in front of you as a patient with my breast rotting under my nose?'

So what I did I went to the PCT, Primary Care Trust, because they have an office in the town where I live and I went and I let my aroma do the talking. (*She laughs.*)

If I as a nurse, a graduate nurse – BSc, a diploma in professional studies, SEN, RGN, midwife – is having problems getting stuff . . . What is it with Joe Bloggs and Mrs Joe Bloggs, couldn't do as I did and stand in front of the mirror and pack my own wounds.

But the practice nurse helped me out a few times and she said, 'You're getting exhausted, Marjorie.' 'Well,' I said, 'I'm so exhausted because I'm being the patient and the nurse here, sometimes I want to give nurse a day off because I'm knackered here.'

And she did a few dressings and she said, 'I'm going to get district nurse to come and see you over weekend Marjorie just to give you a helping hand. Damn it, if we can't help our own, Marjorie, what are we all about?'

The bleeps and commotion of a large supermarket.
The NHS Regulator appears with a shopping trolley.

NHS Regulator You will hear doctors complaining that, you know, every patient I see now thinks they're an expert 'cause they've Googled their symptoms before they come and see me, and they just turn up and say, I need X, Y, Z drug.

Jonathon appears with a trolley.

Jonathon It's so confused now, with the kind of post-modern thing – like we don't know whether we are supposed to trust doctors or not supposed to trust doctors.

NHS Regulator Choice. Well there are two reasons for having choice. One is it's the thing that creates the competitive pressure . . . under certain circumstances, on providers, hospitals for example, to do a better job.

So if you, if I can go to this new hospital that is dedicated at doing cataract surgery, and has a reputation for doing it very well, has got a short waiting list, or I can go to this NHS hospital which doesn't have quite the same reputation and has a long waiting list, and I choose to go with this one, then the NHS hospital is gonna have to ask itself, can we do better?

Jonathon So you're a perfectly healthy young man with a hernia – okay, you might just want to go to a hernia centre.

NHS Regulator If you are gonna have a cataract operation, it's not an emergency, you, you've got time to look around, and you've got a choice between this hospital with certain, you know, it's in a certain location, it may be easier or more difficult to get to, it may have a good reputation, it may not, than that one over there.

Jonathon Where's the best place to go for people who aren't really sure what's wrong with them and they're really, really sick?

The thing about choice, is that it assumes that healthcare is a series of discrete episodes – like illness, diagnosis, treatment, cure – bong! – got it.

NHS Regulator I think you feel more empowered if you've got that choice. Even if at the end of the day if you finish up going to the same hospital you would've done if you hadn't had the choice.

Jonathon So this consumer model of discrete episodes with a beginning and an end might have been suited to the 1948 model of care, where you had your heart attack – you either survived or you died. You got your infection, and you survived or you died. You got your cancer, and you survived or you died. Now, you have your cancer – it's in remission, it comes back, you have your chemotherapy. You have your heart attack, you're treated, you've got heart failure – you're on a treatment for that. You develop emphysema or bronchitis – you're on a treatment for that. You're pretty depressed – you're on a treatment for that. These things all interact. You don't die from any of them.

It's a continual sort of struggle to manage something, rather than an intervention which will cure something, which is what it used to be sixty years ago.

They both disappear into the ward.
We find Peter Bamford watching his son sleeping in a hospital bed. He takes out a printed pamphlet and talks to us.

Peter January 1988 this was written. And it's called *Britain's Biggest Enterprise: Ideas for Radical Reform of the NHS* by Oliver Letwin and John Redwood. They wrote it when they worked for the Centre for Policy Studies.

So, anyway they kind of describe five sort of steps, what it would take to privatise the health service. Here we are.

He goes through the five steps.

So, 'Establishment of the NHS as an independent trust. Increase of the joint ventures between the NHS and the private sector. Extending the principle of charging. System for health credits, and then a national insurance scheme.'

So we've done. We've now got Foundation Trusts and they're all independent and they're all sort of stand-alone from a financial position in theory. You know, (*reading*) 'Increase joint ventures between the NHS and private sector,' well that's certainly happening. (*He reads.*) 'Extending the principle of charging,' well that's . . . It's that whole principle of . . . you know there'll always be something that's available on the NHS but it'll become less and less. If you've got cataracts now, a lot of trusts will only treat one eye . . . Well, if you want both you can pay for the other one!

So (*going on reading*) 'A system of this sort would be fraught with traditional difficulties. It would be foolhardy to move so far from the present in one single step. But need there be just one step, question mark? Might it not rather be possible to work slowly from the present system towards a national insurance scheme . . .' And if that isn't the most dishonest piece . . . Well, actually to give them credit, they were actually open, completely open about this in 1988.

They put it in black and white and said this is what we're proposing. Ever since then it's been completely buried. Not one party has stood on a platform of 'These are the principles, this is our road map for what we're going to do with the NHS – vote for us and we'll implement it.'

I mean it's what tipped me over the edge it . . . I don't want my kids to have sleepless nights when their children are ill, about whether they can afford it and whether they can afford the best treatment or whether they're just going to have to put up with one cataract operation because it's all they can afford. I just don't think – I think we've screwed that generation over enough without leaving them with a legacy of a . . . you know, a skeleton of an NHS.

He goes back to his sleeping son.
Jim appears. The present.

Jim You look at the crisis this Christmas, which was very profound actually, in fact I'm surprised it didn't blow up more, because hospitals were frightened this year.

Cos they had more patients than they knew what to do with. But it wasn't people with nothing wrong with them coming through 111. It was sick old people.

Anita, an economist, appears.

Anita In December, about three-quarters of NHS Acute Hospitals were in deficit.

Jonathon appears.

Jonathon That's Anita, an economist.

Anita And the deficit so far this year is about eight hundred and sixty million pounds. And growing.

Ex-NHS Chief Exec Managed decline, is how I would describe it, that's what it would be. It won't fall over straight away, because, you know, people will work hard. It's like now, in some hospitals, people are working enormous hours to make things happen, because they're committed. And so it won't fall over, in that sense, but it will over time, be managed decline.

Anita So the Treasury gave some extra money in December. And they announced some extra money for next year as well and I think after the election, whoever wins is going to have to find some more money again. Unless people are happy to see either the range or quality of services reduce. There's no sign of that at the moment.

Ex-NHS Chief Exec So my answer is that we're gonna have to pay more money for our healthcare. It's just over 9 per cent of our GDP. In America it's twice higher. But you know, Germany, France, all these places, they pay more for their healthcare, a good 1 or 2 per cent more than we do. And don't forget, they've been doing that for twenty years, not just the last –

Anita Every pound we spend on healthcare . . . It doesn't, the Treasury doesn't have its own money. It comes from all of us.

There's a sense I think for people who believe in the NHS, to my mind, that in addition to calling for more money, they also need to make – there needs to be sort of some humility about the responsibility that comes from this. Every pound we spend badly is care not provided to somebody. That need to make sure that we're always running the system as well as we possibly can is not some dry economic imperative, it's a moral imperative actually.

The ward is stripped back.
Jonathon reappears.

Jonathon Care is hugely important and that's the bit that all the scandals have been over, so the Mid Staffs people not getting washed, not being treated kindly and compassionately, and that's because, I think that's partly because of a culture which is obsessed with fighting illness rather than supporting patients.

A nurse passes through with a cello.

There's a huge disparity between medic doctor power and nurse power, so most of the money and the funding and stuff gets sucked up by the kind of cure end rather than the care end of healthcare, and it would take a huge cultural shift to change that because patients get sucked along with this narrative of battling. You know, the fight against cancer, the fight against heart disease, the fight against, you know and all these different fights going on – 'We're going to win, and we're going to beat them' – but actually you don't.

Another nurse passes through with a violin.

So you need care, you need long-term care and care is about continuity, care is about people, care is not about industry and technological gadgets and highly expensive . . . and all of the kudos and whatnot.

A doctor passes though with a violin.

Healthcare, at least as much now as it was sixty-five years ago, depends on human-relationship-based care and that just doesn't fit with capitalism which is about replacing labour with capital.

A surgeon passes through with a viola.

The economist who wrote about it was a guy called Baumol, who wrote Baumol's *Cost Disease*, he pointed out that it took four people to play a Beethoven string quartet at the time it was written and it still does now.

We hear a Beethoven string quartet.

It still takes as long to train those people to play their instruments and so effectively in healthcare work, what we are trying to do is to get three untrained people who have never played a violin before, or a string instrument, to play a string quartet, that's what we're doing, we're getting healthcare assistants to do the jobs of nurses or nurses to do the job of GPs and iPad's to do the jobs of pharmacists and you know it's going to be as bad as three untrained people trying to play a Beethoven string quartet.

An exhausted Dave, the Brighton paramedic, appears, undoing his coat and shirt. He's just finished his shift – the same shift we saw him head off to at the beginning of the play.

Dave It's the little things in the health service you'll get the thanks for if you've got the time to do it, like holding somebody's hand, *when* they're frightened . . . *They* are the things, the surgeon might do the great big operation but the . . . I guarantee you that it'll be the nurse that's spent time, at the bed, holding hand, holding somebody's hand, that'll get the thanks. And that's the buzz that I get, I wouldn't call it a buzz, I just get the satisfaction . . . At the end of the day that I've made somebody *laugh* . . . Or had a chat with them, or made them a – something, the simple things – or made them a cup of tea, not . . .

The frail old woman appears.

Jonathon Lonely people are twice as likely to go to A&E as non-lonely people. For example, little old lady falls over in the middle of the night, can't get off the floor, rings an ambulance to take her to A&E. It's nice and warm and sunny and everyone's lovely, they make her a cup of tea and talk to her. Nobody's made her a cup of tea or talked to her since she last went to A&E six weeks ago.

Jonathon takes the frail old woman by the hand and leads her off.

Marjorie You see, I'll pick up on, I'll be sent to do an ECG, somebody with chest pain and things like that. So obviously I'll engage with the patient! As I'm putting on my twelve leads and things like that. And you'll be, 'Have you had this before, is there something bothering you at home or at work or whatever?' And then, yes, they've been getting chest pain because they've been getting themselves into debt, they've been losing jobs, you know, and things. Or there's been a cutback, now they're doing two people's jobs. It definitely is reflecting and with more presentations with chest pain and it being a stress related . . .

When you're stressed out you're – (*she breathes a short breath*) you're not using the full chest capacity, you're not using the . . . not inflating the whole of the lungs – (*she does short breaths*) you're tending to use upper chest and it can affect the internal biochemistry, upskittle biochemistry can temporarily constrict the coronary arteries supplying the muscle, so it gives you a pseudo-angina, so as if you're having . . . Whereas if you sort out your breathing . . .

A lot of people will go, 'Do deep breathing,' they'll go, 'Take a deep breath,' but that is actually the wrong way. Think of how the yogis do it and how these masters do it, it's what I used to teach with my women getting through their contractions. 'Concentrate on the outwards breath first,' because what you want to do is empty out the breath that is already in the lungs, and in that, visualise letting out all the negativity and all the pain and the discomfort, just letting that go, because you don't even have to think about the inward breath because physics will sort that out. You've emptied out, so air will automatically come in. So it's less energy you're expending if you concentrate on breathing out. (*She does a slow out-breath.*) Yeah?

End.